PRIME GREEN:
REMEMBERING
THE
SIXTIES

ecco

An Imprint of HarperCollins*Publishers*

PRIME GREEN: REMEMBERING THE SIXTIES

ROBERT STONE

HarperCollins books may be purchased for educational, business, or sales promotional use. For information, please write: Special Markets Department, HarperCollins Publishers, 10 East 53rd Street, New York, NY 10022.

Portions of this work have appeared, in slightly different form, in *The New Yorker*, *Playboy*, and *Narrative*.

All photographs courtesy of the author, unless otherwise noted.

Photographs on middle insert pages and back cover, as indicated, taken by Ronald Bevirt, "Merry Prankster" Hassler, who lives in Eugene, Oregon. 2007 Copyright Ronald Bevirt. All Rights Reserved.

FIRST EDITION

Designed by Jessica Shatan Heslin

Library of Congress Cataloging-in-Publication Data

Prime green : remembering the sixties / Robert Stone.
p. cm.

ISBN: 978-0-06-019816-9
ISBN-10: 0-06-019816-8

Stone, Robert, 1937–. Authors, American—20th century—Biography. Nineteen sixties.

PS3569.T6418 Z47 2007
813'.54 B 22   2006046351

07   08   09   10   11   WBC/CW   10   9   8   7   6   5   4   3   2   1

With love and gratitude for the
enduring friendships of that time,
and to those, living or gone,
who shared what we saw
and what we were

PRIME GREEN: REMEMBERING THE SIXTIES

ONE

In 1958 I was on the bridge of the USS *Arneb,* an ungainly naval transport ship with the lines of a tramp steamer. LCVPs were stacked on hatches fore and aft under mammoth A-frames designed to raise and lower them. The *Arneb* had entertained kamikazes at Okinawa. Veterans of Normandy and the South Pacific ran many of the ship's divisions.

That quarter of 1957–58, spring in the Northern calendar, darkening autumn in the Southern Ocean, we had been given some kind of pass from the alerts of the cold war. UNESCO had designated 1958 as an International Geophysical Year and the Navy had patched together the *Arneb* as America's contibution. We were tracking electrical activity on the surface of the sun, "sunspots" in the far south of the Indian Ocean, southwest of the ghost whaling station on the Crozet Islands. On board was a team of astrophysicists from the University of Chicago. It was the last of the Antarctic expeditions mapped out by Admiral Richard Byrd and was known as Operation Deep Freeze III.

One day we were steaming on the northern edge of the ice floes at the latitude where the seasonal oscillations of the Antarctic Convergence determine the weather. The subpolar wind warmed as it quickened, the dark blue plain of ocean rising into spiky horsetails that here and there showed white. The weather in the far south, I was learning, was weird and contrary in ways that made it differ from the Arctic. April at latitude 55 offered a dark sapphire sky dappled with cirrus trails. Colors were harsh and dry, without mist. Icebergs flashed on the horizons, intensely defined yet somehow ghostly, like hallucinations.

I was at the helm, a watch where the night hours looked little different from day. The ocean glowed with the same strangely referred light. As a petty officer (my rank was officially journalist third class) I was exempt from helm watches. In fact I enjoyed them far out at sea. A watch on the helm on the open ocean involved keeping an eye on the binnacle indicator, feeling the big lumbering transport fall away under the roaring polar wind, then bringing her back on so that the needle showed the designated course. A helmsman got to know the ship and its eccentricities, its stubborn lists and rolls. If the captain or the exec had not planned some exercise for the day, it was a soothing routine.

The formalities of the bridge were vaguely liturgical: terse commands repeating ancient formulas in antique language, bells, blocks of Morse code reporting weather from the adjoining radio shack, the boatswain's whistle at the regulation times of day. There was a sense of everything seriously in place. Over and over, we located and re-aligned ourselves in the mathematics of the planet, forever adjusting and correcting the location of our tuck in space and time. The ocean around us stood for blue infinity. Time came to us courtesy of the Naval Observatory, sifting out across the garden fifteen thousand miles away in Washington, over which Vice President Nixon then brooded.

Also, helm watches could be traded for other, less diverting details in the ship's system of graft and barter. The duty helmsman whose watch I stood would perform some equivalent responsibility for me. With the ship far out at sea, the helmsman's sole responsibility was to keep the ship on course, so there was time for daydreaming.

For the previous month or so we had been undergoing repairs in Melbourne. In the antipodean autumn of 1958, I spent my idle hours contemplating the moves of an Australian Olympic fencer named Denise Corcoran, whom I had met by carrying her foils across Hyde Park, the one in Sydney. I had learned something from Denise, and I was still grappling with the substance of it.

Crossing Hyde Park, Denise and I found that we were both bound for Melbourne: the *Arneb* was going in for repairs to its evaporator system; Denise was headed for hours of swordplay in a gymnasium above the Spencer Street railroad station, preparing for the Empire Games that were due to start in Montreal in a few months.

I went often to watch her work in the dingy gym above the station, even when we had settled down together (on our free nights at least) in a mean and ugly neighborhood at the end of the line. She was tall and redheaded, which she told me was all wrong for fencers; it aroused anger and spite in opponents because you looked, as she put it, like a big gawk—people laughed. Fencers were meant to be compact and sleek, never outsized, overdone, or obvious, certainly not freckled and redheaded and slightly bucktoothed like my Denise. Nevertheless, she seemed to be their star, intimidating the other girls. Out on the ocean, in my mind's eye, I could still see how she used the long, strong, and shapely legs she complained about in unexpected lunges that ran her enemy the length of the enclosure. The fencer's costume was particularly lacking in any sort of glamour, but she could appear quite handsome and provocative, planted and prepared to strike. I liked the way the cloth of her breeches wrinkled over the taut skin at the backs of her knees. I also enjoyed her pretense to a complete absence of humor, which made her a most droll comic. She used expressions like "crikey," "fair dinkum," and "truly." A pint made her "squiffed."

Some days, if I had a twenty-four in town, I would sneak Denise early out of the gym, out from under the raptor dragon gaze of her coach. This meant making our way through the humid halls and moist saloons and beer-polished private lounges of the vast station in which around five o'clock each afternoon a state of headlong societal breakdown was under way. In those days the official bar-closing hour in the state of Victoria was 6 p.m. (It was the bloody women, blokes explained—they had the vote, they wanted the blokes home for their tea.) At the same time, the general hour at which the clerks and shop assistants and bookkeepers of the City were relieved of their day's employment was 5:30. Thousands of wage slaves raged out of Melbourne's Victorian brownstone office buildings and headed for the Spencer Street station. Most of them wanted a drink.

At the bars around the station it was frantic. One place in the cellar served its vigorous tawny beer through a hose; customers thrust their pint glasses forth and stood to withstand the spray. Admiring

Australians as I do, I continue to think their prohibitionist impulses of that time were excessive and misguided. Such impulses usually are. The floors were puddled with beer and sick. There were fights. And there was the business of conducting young Denise, all decked out for sport, through the hordes while preserving the inviolability of her person.

Of course the scene was rowdy and aggressively macho, but the Australian dimension provided a sometimes prevailing good humor and a tolerant sense of absurdity. This ceremonial was the Aussie answer to what one of the French decadents called *L'Heure Jaune,* the "Yellow Hour," when, a hundred years ago, one took absinthe on St. Germain. It was called locally "the swirl," pronounced with the most inimitable array of diphthongs this side of Pittsburgh.

In the six weeks we spent refitting in Christchurch, Sydney, and Melbourne I had a lesson on the subject of being or not being American. Australians and New Zealanders in the fifties felt very positively about Americans, felt a degree of kinship in blood and language that the desperate struggle with Japan had strengthened. This of course is history, and history's narratives are being revised to suit our sorry times. But even when the people of the two southern commonwealths admired the United States and rejoiced in the alliance, they had no particular intention of emulating its ways. Denise among others explained the differences between the U.S. and other lands, most of which neither of us had ever seen.

One night we spent a cultural evening at Melbourne's only cinematic art house, watching a film of the Bolshoi Ballet's production of *Giselle.* Denise cried. Maybe it was because she wasn't a dancer and desired to be. Maybe it was at the sheer crepuscular Transylvanian morbidness of the show. Anyway, she wept wholesome tears on my neckerchief. I thought she was falling in love with me, to the extent that I understood the phrase, much less the thing itself. I imagined that I felt the same way. We were both transported by this weirdly colored dance film portraying the effect of class distinctions on wisps and wilis. It had nice music and I had nice Denise beside me in her party pants and freckles. It was all fantasy but the inexpert merging, back in St. Kilda.

Denise, unlike many young middle-class women in Australia, had no self-consciousness about being seen with American sailors. We dreamed. With my political sophistication, instinct for strategy, and brilliant navigation, coupled with Denise's swordsmanship and fearlessness, the Indies lay at our feet. We might strike out for the throne of a rajah or Borneo. However, as we drank to love and the Southern Cross and the beer-blighted sky over Melbourne, we began to argue about, of all things, national character and how it might interfere with our plans. Somehow we reached the point of Americans Worship the Dollar.

"Americans worship the dollar," Denise told me.

I was shocked. "Who worships the dollar? Me?"

I was the only child of a single New York schoolteacher. I had grown up in an SRO hotel room she had maintained on her tiny disability payments. Poverty was part of my identity at that time. I romanticized and sentimentalized it.

"Well, not you so much," Denise assured me, and she took my hand in her strong grasp. "You're an artistic type."

This assessment in Australia was not necessarily a compliment.

"What the hell does that mean?"

"It shows in your hands." She took hold of my right hand in her trained grip. "You have long sensitive fingers. Not like most blokes."

I let that one pass.

"Money's all they think about," she said sadly. "Isn't it? Yanks? Money and sex?"

"Sailors don't have any money." It occurred to me they had not much sex either.

"I don't mean you. You don't count."

"It's just a cliché," I complacently explained. "One of many anti-American clichés around."

"Everyone says you all get paid too much."

"To buy you gin with, darling girl."

She told me I had said a rotten thing. She would buy her own. She also told me I could ask anyone about Americans and their passion for money. It wasn't something she'd made up.

We managed to put the subject aside. On my way back to the *Arneb* the next morning I began to ponder Denise's reflections.

It was true that people in Anzac land rarely talked about money or their jobs. I had learned the then current sterling monetary system playing poker in Christchurch in the homes of people who had stopped their cars to invite me to dinner. I was hopeless at telling half crowns from ha'pennies and equally hopeless at poker, but I could not stop my hosts from letting me win. And no one ever volunteered what they did for a living. It was not something people talked about.

On my way home to the ship, it occurred to me that recently major league baseball had been traumatized when the owners of the Brooklyn Dodgers and the New York Giants left their longtime supporters to the wind through their crumbling stadium walls, decamping to the sleek West. As they went they left the chumps with the inside story: that nothing American men did was more important than making money.

Denise was an athlete possessed of a certain spiritual certainty. I suddenly realized that this toothy little jock from the ends of the earth knew a few things that I, a New York boy, didn't. She was on my mind a lot. We wrote. By the time of the Empire Games I would be out of the Navy and we might meet in Montreal.

I was drifting between our course and the prospect of Canadian autumn when the starboard lookout reported a vessel moving parallel with our course. Presently the captain appeared on the bridge and ordered the special sea and anchor detail to stations. I handed over the wheel to the quartermaster of the watch.

For the next fifteen minutes we watched the long blue-black line stretch out at a slight angle of interception to our course. It seemed to stretch without limit, as far as the after horizon, where the sun was declining, threatening to disappear. We must have overtaken it, because the faster the speed we made, the farther the long line stretched out ahead of us.

The captain was a gloomy man, a disappointed career officer lacking any sense of what European social critics call deep play, the disinterested spirit of serious fun they claim Americans so often lack. They were right about the Old Man. He had been demoted, as he saw it, from the destroyer Navy to our grim gray amphibs for some violation of the tin can code. But apparently the great beast on our horizon intrigued him, too. He ordered the ship to starboard in the direction of the mass. The grizzled quartermaster of the watch kept a baleful eye on him. Presumably he knew what the Old Man had done to cashier himself from the destroyer Navy.

Captain H., splendid in his bridge coat, raised his binoculars and studied the mass that was keeping speed with us at half a mile's distance.

"Unidentified vessel," he declared, "proceeding west on bearing . . ." He let the bearing go. The quartermaster recorded our position.

The vessel the captain thought he saw was low in the water and was certainly proceeding west. Whatever engine powered it was mysterious to me; it seemed to throb, a distinctly unstable mass. At this distance we could see that there were flights of predatory birds attending it, mainly the terrible buzzard gulls called skuas.

Watching the captain, on whose observations and decisions we all depended, I suddenly suspected that he was going to give the order to fire. Not that we had much to fire with: a five-inch deck gun and a fifty-caliber machine gun only our single gunner's mate could work. But the captain was not some kind of trigger-happy savage compelled to make a target of anything that could float. It was my imagination entirely.

Still, the destroyer sailor's impulse was to at least line up unidentified craft as targets. It was something of a trick to sail an eleven-knot cargo ship with two operative guns as though it were a destroyer, but in that regard the Old Man had some imagination too. He displayed his nostalgia for tin cans by trying to hold gunnery practice with our five-inch after cannon. The gun stood near the fantail under a canvas cover. Two gunner's mates or strikers manned it, plus the sight setter (often me), in a regular attempt to pulverize a target balloon. In the subantarctic sea the winds could easily blow at ninety knots, and the target balloon would come out of the box, pick up the prevailing breeze, and disappear over the horizon before anyone could manage to say "Fire!" or even think it. The echoing boom of the five-inch resounded in memory of the target balloon, which by then had probably been claimed as a beach toy by laughing girls in Cape Town. If I was the sight setter and had forgotten my gloves at the call to battle stations, I would find myself halfway up the steel ladder to the sight mechanism, my fingers securely frozen to a steel rung of the ladder. I was without guilt; our chances of hitting the balloon were null. However, I was something of a discrepancy in the rigging, an "Irish pennant" as the Navy said, standing halfway to the crow's nest while the deck pitched and rolled far below.

———

Relieved of the wheel, I stayed on the bridge, hoping not to be noticed and ordered to occupy myself with something useful. I shared a pair of binoculars with the bridge messenger and watched the mass in front of us change shape and direction while we adjusted course to make way for it. The longer I looked at the thing, the more awesome it seemed. It looked formless, but we could see that it was plainly alive. In my mind at least it assumed a sort of monstrousness, a living thing huge and strong, unrecognizable.

"Penguins," someone said. It may have been one of our learned scientists, wandered up from his stateroom.

Penguins they were, Adélie penguins, the little hooded characters who waddle clownishly around their breeding colonies. The book on Adélie penguins will tell you that they are "ungainly" on land and that, having no land-based enemies, they have little fear of man; encountering humans, they pause to regard them "quizzically." Their Chaplin-like gait and myopic, clueless stares deprive them of the dignity to which all creatures in their natural state should be entitled. Even the desperate defense of their nests and eggs has an absurd quality. They come at the persistent intruder, cackling Donald Duck–like, fowl obscenities and churning their flippers faster than the eye can see, like so many tasteful little pinball machine components. A good shot with the flipper, however, can buy them back a little respect, since they're capable of breaking a human's leg with one, and they give it all the force a small ridiculous bird can muster. But on land they are among nature's comedians. Nature, pretty humorless in tooth and claw, provides few.

The Adélie's transformation in the grip of its migratory instinct, from droll oddity to mighty exemplar of the life force, is one of the great sights the ocean affords a traveler, one of the runic lessons you go on considering for the rest of your life. At different stages of your life they seem to vary in the substance of their meaning. And they *do signify,* provide a glimpse into the nature of things, or what the Roman poet so eloquently called "the tears of things." As someone once said, everything that's true about the ocean is true about life in general in some way, small or great. For me, most of these insights had something to do with the ocean.

For an hour, the men on the bridge of the USS *Arneb* watched this enormous colony of penguins proceed. They swam *porpoising,* in very long graceful curves which for all I know might have been perfect. Their strength in swimming and diving is quite disproportional to their size; diving they descend to more than six hundred feet to search for the tiny crustaceans called krill that make up most of their diet.

The Adélie arrive at their breeding grounds in October and nest on the Antarctic mainland. By the austral fall, the young penguins are old enough to make the migration we were seeing, from their rocky beaches on shore to shelf ice or any other convenient surface at the edge of the Antarctic Convergence, the edge of polar summer weather. For what it's worth, we now know, as we did not then, that the Adélie's winter breeding grounds are pitched farther and farther south as the average winter temperature increases.

Later that night as the sun dipped to the tip of the nearest icebergs, the winds picked up, and by 0600 they were near the top of
the Beaufort scale. The penguins stayed with us, sharing passages
between the floes, porpoising on as though they had a chosen destination in their collective birdy mind. We had slowed to let the sonar
read us through the icebergs. The wind was on our starboard quarter, and the ship had a chronic port list. When I went below to
crash, taking to my rack, which was the highest of a four-high tier, I
lay back to read with my pocket flashlight. I had *Ulysses* out of the
Norfolk, Virginia, public library and plenty of time to be patient
with it. When we'd start sliding to port, I'd stay with Leopold
Bloom as long as I could tough it out, waiting for the big lumbering
ship to arrest its roll and come back to starboard. In rough weather,
it seemed as though it would never make it back, that we were about
to slide down through a crushing, sodden world and down the
whole deep six. At such times I would set my book aside and turn
off my light and ponder fortune. An old master-at-arms I knew had
advice for sinking sailors: "Be grateful you're not burning." A little
gratitude and a glance at the bright side might ease one's passage,
the old man thought. But we came back every time, lumbered back
up to ride the next forward motion, as I stared at the red light over
the watertight door and silently cheered the big canoe's comeback.
It occurred to me at one of those moments that I was happier than I
had ever been before—with the penguins, the icebergs, the Beaufort
scale, and the celestial nimbus clouds cruising above the wind. And
happier, I suspected, than I would ever be again.

Operation Deep Freeze III brought with it a variety of jobs for
me. At one point I helped count penguins, which brought me a lifetime of insomnia in black and white. I interviewed members of the
ship's crew ashore so that the jabbering creatures—the penguins

mainly—could play as background in the recruiting commercials on their hometown radio stations. I stamped letters for collectors with Antarctic postmarks, sorted the mail, put out a four-page daily newspaper, and spun a little jazz disc jockey show during dinner hour. I remember some of our featured platters: Kai Winding and J. J. Johnson at Ronnie Scott's. We had Keely Smith with Louis Prima at the Cal-Neva Lodge. Before each number Prima would announce a dedication to Sam Giancana, who owned the place and was apparently present for Keely's performances. Things like this, like the copy of *On the Road* that was one of my other traveling books, now seem to have served as portents of the life and the world that lay ahead of us. From time to time I faced the mathematical mysteries of the five-inch gun's sight. To justify my top-secret clearance, I did up a little intelligence report for the captain and the intelligence officer. This was basically the news of the day, beefed up with some intercepts that were encoded in blocks of five characters.

I counted my one intelligence coup when, from our station at Cape Hallett, we visited the Soviet ice station at Mirny. Instructed to "have a look around," I never focused beyond the first vodka. I don't think my opposite number among the Russian party made it past the first gift copy of *Playboy* that we gave him. The Russians received their *Playboy*s in an attitude that began with condescending chuckles, eased into superior smiles, and soon tightened in lascivious concentration. They made no comments to us, or to each other. In fact they neglected to thank us. Nevertheless they seemed grateful, and when we started north they asked for more.

Everyone was multitasking, but the Antarctic tasks were relieved by beach time. Our next liberty port was Durban, in the province of Natal, South Africa, and our beach time there came with another portent.

The South African police appeared at the pier to enforce a segregated liberty policy. Maybe they didn't behave like storm troopers, but that's how I remember them. I really do remember the humiliation I felt, that many of us felt, at being subjected to inspection by these sneering, sunburned headbreakers. Over the week we spent in Durban we heard continually that the police delighted in enforcing the sexual segregation law, whatever it was called, on foreigners—that the first offense for a foreigner was four or five decades breaking rocks in the Kalahari. It was a story worked up to terrorize sailors over the years. The authorities seemed obsessed.

In Cape Town the year before, after the last Operation Deep Freeze, Filipinos had counted as "Europeans" and were sent on their way toward the pier exit signs that read "Europeans Only." But here in Durban, an English-speaking city, with a British colonial vibe, Filipinos were considered nonwhites. They were consigned to the class of humankind for which the South African police and some people in the U.S. Navy reserved short, spitty, ugly words that come straight from the amygdala. White South Africa had about the ugliest and most degrading versions of that wounding utterance: they called a victim of their racism *munt*. Measure the word's weight and intensity by remembering that a man who calls you a "munt" will kill you.

Memory manipulated can clean up our act and help us feel better about ourselves than we deserve. Though I remember with some pride my outrage at my shipmates, American sailors, being subjected to this insolence, I cannot remember saying or doing anything about it in public. I might not have gone ashore. However, I did. That it never occurred to me to refuse a liberty in the name of decency, to deny myself the chance of seeing South Africa, troubles my recollections, colors everything that I recall about South Africa.

I do remember thinking: How can the American government let this happen? And sure enough, the next day black and Filipino sailors who had not previously experienced one of the Navy's goodwill visits to South Africa returned from the locations to which they had been bused for entertainment variously knifed, shot, and scalded with acid, and to a man robbed. They spent the rest of our week in port safely aboard. I had the option of staying aboard too in solidarity. I didn't. I saw myself as a sympathetic outsider in the business, a man of progressive instincts ready to observe South African racism with disapproval. The second day of liberty in Durban the American diplomatic community decided to make a policy of entertaining visiting American sailors at their homes. So my sympathy, my progressive instincts and readiness to act upon them, proved to be one day behind those of President Eisenhower's State Department.

We had fun, we who went ashore. We had long thoughtful conversations with Indian functionaries and servants who made it plain that they expected the present regime to last no more than twenty years. Some of them told us that Indians would no doubt be driven out of the country at the time of African liberation.

We called up the women's dorm at the University of Natal and made a blind date with three young women. Two were South Africans, and one was an American from Portuguese East Africa whose father was a nomadic oil executive and who lived a life a little like an Army brat's.

Being in the presence of a great crime always manages to arouse competing moral perspectives from the sentient witnesses. Apartheid made me and my shipmates superior to the Natal college students because they seemed to us to be defending it. Of course they were, summoning as many ironies and contradictions from their experiences as they could in support of the intellectually and morally vacuous apartheid system, citing exceptionalist and anecdotal mitigating circumstances connected with their friends and family. These stories from the cozy, cheery side of apartheid—which they denied defending—were of great significance to the young women. White South Africans, addressing the outside world, addressing each other, clung to small contrarian myths that would be swept away by history.

I had a strange feeling in Natal that the English South Africans often assumed they were accepted as opponents of apartheid, while everything they said seemed to prove they preferred it to any imaginable alternative. They, and to some extent Indians and Zulus as well, saw their relationship to the system as jury-rigged and temporary.

After a few days of scrutiny, of being told by every street tout and bartender that the police were hard on our trail and watching our every move, we underwent an attack of lawlessness.

The street along the beachfront, called the Marine Parade, offered a feature unique to the beaches of Natal. Zulu men in full regalia, with leopard robes and lion-tooth necklaces, arrows and assegais, pulled brightly colored rickshaws, conducting tourists past the grand old-fashioned porches of the seaside hotels. On all the porches elderly white couples sat rocking, gentlemen with imperial mustaches, ladies in white hats with green shaded crowns, all watching the traffic on the Marine Parade with general disapproval. Walking past them in our dress whites, we were made to feel we had failed to win their approval. Hotel staff stood at the gates in case we decided to enter where we weren't wanted, ready to suggest a different establishment, a different parade.

Stopping one of the Zulu rickshaw men, we talked him into taking a seat in the back. Then my friend Galen and I each picked up a blade of the rickshaw and ran headlong down the Marine Parade, giving the geezers another chance to love us. There were bells and whistles and police Klaxons. We found that the rickshaw was capable of great speed, and having thrown our shoulders into the takeoff, we were hauling the Zulu down the street at a velocity beyond our control. We had created a dreadful spectacle that unleashed chaos on the once pleasant street. The pensioners at the hotels were not happy with the awfulness unfolding, nor were Galen and I, who had totally lost control of the conveyance, which threatened to outrun us and carry our passenger off the adjoining cliffs and into the shark-infested breakers below. And by far, it was the Zulu bearer himself who was least amused by this reversal; he clung to the side of the rickshaw and shouted things like "Bollocks!" and "Piss off!" and *"Stop!"*

Finally we succeeded in stopping the awful thing and assisted our victim onto the sidewalk.

"Oh me," he said. "Bollocks you."

We gave him money. If no one had stopped us we would have given money to the geezers on the porch and to the black auxiliary policemen who arrived to philosophize about events. Overtipping the rickshaw man made me think of F. Scott Fitzgerald's bitter line about Americans buying their way in and out of various antics with their money. "If you wanted real snow," he wrote, "you gave someone some money."

My friend Galen was a literary type with no more than one grand theft auto behind him in the street and one anchor tattoo on his forearm. One of the sort of guys I hung out with. Types like Galen and me were the Navy's foreign legionnaires: high school dropouts without much family, a history of petty crimes, and a lot of autodidact lore. When our time got short, as mine and Galen's was, the Navy got nervous about us. We were hard to bully and quite taken with what might be called the Navy's funny side. There we were in Africa.

"The horror," Galen said to remind us. "The horror."

There were legendary fuckups by visiting American sailors in foreign ports which made their impact on history. Maybe a couple of wise guys blew up the *Maine,* screwing with flares. In any case, wandering sailors have often been the trigger of unfortunate incidents. A liberty section of a ship I was aboard decided to attend evening prayers at one of Izmir's principal mosques. It was terrifying to watch. The sailors, overcome with bogus piety, kept trying to get their supplicant bows in step with those of the Turkish worshippers, and failing. One guy passed out; another yelled for Jesus. Today, I suppose, these guys would be decorating a traffic signal in some godly town. But in those days the young Turks laughed. Crowded against the ironwork windows, watching the drunk American sailors attempt devotion, kids and teenagers and passing Turkish sailors laughed themselves sick. Izmir, Turkey, 1956. Such events boded ill for the future, but at that time people seemed amused and tolerant.

And I don't think the sailors in the mosque were hostile to Islam.

For my own part I once pissed on the temple of the Olympian Zeus. Funny how often profanation by urine comes into it. Street stuff. But this was in Athens, mind you, and the Olympian Zeus's temple was a Roman construction meant to demonstrate the naturalization and subordination of the Greek pantheon to the Roman; the seated Zeus was Jupiter. I felt no filial guilt.

Cold war troops, we were not impressed by the non-American world. I once asked a veteran boatswain's mate what the Mediterranean ports were like.

"Like everything over there," he said. "Crummy. Fucked up."

That wasn't my view, though mine was equally meretricious. I pulled all the strings I could find to get leave to go to a bullfight in Málaga. I was ecstatic over every instant; not one of Hemingway's recommended emotions did I leave unexperienced. Olé.

Some committed Navy philistines cheered for the bull, but mainly the liberty party behaved itself.

I had seen the things I'd read about. Crossing the Atlantic for the first time, I was on radio watch, carrying the message board around the ship. From the bridge I saw the sun come up over the Rock of Gibraltar.

In the Strait of Malacca, I saw the thousand little ringed lights of the fishing-pirate junks of the Malay sea people. Picking past their craft we heard their flutes and bells. It was a faraway ocean but was what I'd come for.

Passing the Lipari Islands headed for Beirut we passed between Scylla and Charybdis. From the peak of Stromboli great rich salvos of flaming molten rock were tossed in the smoky air. The ocean smelled of the Malvasia grapes that grew on the slope.

Once, at Ismailia, I nearly got to fire the five-inch in anger. It was October 1956 and we were evacuating American civilians from the Suez Canal Zone. Mystère jets from the French carrier *Lafayette* were bombing the harbor areas, sending donkeys and baskets of figs and women wrapped in folds of cloth high in the air. Coming in, the planes would seem to be touching our radar masts. We had a huge American flag with spotlights on it. Our position was helpless, tied up at what they call Med Mole, a system of docking used in many Mediterranean ports, where the fantail of the ship is up against the pierside and a boat runs to the landing station. Each time a plane came over we would awkwardly track it with our five-inch and our fifty-caliber, waiting for the order to fire, really wanting to hear it. American sailors have been known to die by mistake in the Middle East, usually victims of Israeli fire forgetting its friendliness for a few hours. But we in the amphib Navy were ready to start our own little naval war with France. It would, I think, have been the second. But fortunately none of our civilians were hurt and the French were bluffing. Egyptians died, though, begging us for protection, and we were moored close enough to them to take it personally. A general rage spread among all hands, a rage of battle I had never seen before.

I had to be grateful for all that. I was. I was not going to forget the migrating birds in the Indian Ocean or Mount Erebus smoking.

Or the human factors: my fatuousness, as I reflected more and more on it. More than anything I was to remember the people, the Australians and New Zealanders as they were fifty years ago, the variety of young Americans to be found in the Navy, recruited from pretelevision America, a place more varied than younger people today imagine.

On July 14, 1958, I walked toward the main gate of the Naval Operations Base at Norfolk, Virginia. I had a manila envelope with my discharge in my hand.

I turned a corner and saw a huge carrier tied up at the berth closest to the pier. It was the French carrier *Lafayette,* the ship with which we had come close to exchanging fire in November 1956. The French sailors at attention on deck were elegantly squared away, the ship and the aircraft spotless. A band on the flight deck was playing "La Marseillaise"; my heart rose in my breast. That day I had no beef with the French. I had seen some sights and even learned a few things in the Navy. The import of most of the lessons would take years to dawn clear for me. I felt very worldly, but in fact my international sophistication was severely limited.

TWO

I had missed New York with a passion during my time in the Navy. During our global voyage on the *Arneb* I'd kept two photographs over my desk: one of the Manhattan skyline as it looked just after World War II and one of Brigitte Bardot. These were the poles of my desire.

I had been on a minority enlistment in the service, which meant that, joining before my eighteenth birthday, I would get out—or at least into the reserves—on or about my twenty-first birthday. Around the time of my release I was only beginning to understand how time worked, and how lives registered their passage. Things seemed to happen faster; changes came more and more quickly.

The Navy I'd joined contained many young men who had never seen a television set in a private home. I was one of them. I was also a New York boy; I had never owned a car and couldn't drive. American regions and their cultures had come out of isolation during the Second World War, but there were only radio and movies to further homogenization. Or sometimes to resist it. In 1955, authentic country music, pitched to the white South, rarely employed a drum. Rock and roll was coming. It would change everything. One Sunday in the summer of 1955, a cook at the Naval Training Station, Bainbridge, Maryland, had the idea to serve his recruits pizza as a treat. He advertised it as pizza pie. Back where most of these men came from, pie was festively served with ice cream. Predictably, more than half of them put their ice cream on it. It wouldn't have happened three and a half years later, by which time America had been sold various versions of what was supposed to be pizza, coast to coast.

Regional accents were stronger; diction varied more. People from Appalachia had a dismissive challenge for antagonists: "You and what army? Coxey's?" Coxey's Army was a populist gathering that marched on Washington in William Jennings Bryan's time. American speech carried whispers and echoes of the century before.

There was no old homestead for me to reclaim, just the city. My mother and I had shared a single furnished double room between the time I was eight and the time I joined the Navy at seventeen. When I left for boot camp she moved into one of the pigeon-splattered hotels off Madison Square, a soot-blackened invocation of the Mitteleuropean Beaux-Arts. It looked, under its stained brick, like the only Baedecker-recommended hotel in some Trans-Carpathian provincial capital the Hapsburgs had thoughtlessly annexed.

Among the guests at that time was Colonel Rudolph Ivanovich Abel, a highly respected Soviet spy of the period. There he resided for several years and there he was arrested, to the distress of residents like my mother, who missed his central European good manners and military éclat.

From the week of my discharge, I rented a very small, extremely clean room in the gargantuan St. George Hotel on Clark Street in Brooklyn. The rent for a single sans bath was fifteen dollars a week, which included use of the huge saltwater swimming pool, steam room, and sauna. I had found a job with a magazine in downtown Brooklyn. Every morning I would have a swim and walk to work at the downtown end of Flatbush Avenue.

The magazine that employed me was a civilian-operated magazine designed for naval enlisted men, a struggling antique. Its pages were full of ancient sea stories, like the reminiscences of old salts about their years on the China Station. Correspondents inquired about their lost shipmates aboard gunboats that had long since been knackered for razor blades. Did anyone else out there, subscribers wrote to ask, remember the Lucky Pussycat Bar off the Bund in old Shanghai?

An ad ran in every issue, unaltered since the twenties, that promoted a still popular brand of shoe polish. Its artwork featured the drawing of a good-humored marine, in spats and gleaming boots, kicking a stylized Latino in the behind. On the other side of the page—a sort of "later, that evening" was suggested—the same marine sat at a candlelit table on the plaza, drinking a beer and surrounded by the traditional flashing-eyed señoritas. Their quivering lace fans failed to conceal their admiration and lust for the marine. His shoes shone with a spectral radiance, and beside him another stylized Latino (or perhaps the same one across the page?) awaited the jarhead's pleasure, sombrero in hand, with a toothy, untrustworthy smile. The copy was too offensive to bear recalling—even then, unenlightened as I was, it caused me an inward cringe.

The best thing about the magazine was its location on one of the highest stories of the Williamsburg Bank Building. The bank's tower was an art deco dirigible in unchallenged command of the vast spaces of Brooklyn and beyond. In one direction were the towers of Manhattan and the bridges. In another were the vast fields of Brooklyn that only the dead knew, the cemeteries, abandoned Ebbets Field like a crumbling riverboat, and—on a different quarter—the unbridged Narrows, Coney Island, the Steeplechase, the parachute jump. Beyond these was the Lower Bay, and Sandy Hook and the Atlantic's rollers, a vision "commensurate"—as the great writer said—"to [our] capacity to wonder." I found it also a great inducement to idleness and daydreaming.

Sometimes I thought about Denise. Once I found an item on the Empire Games in Montreal, followed by a small print box with the results of various competitions. Denise was there; she had fenced her way into a place somewhere in the middle of the order. I thought of taking the bus to Montreal, but of course I didn't.

Most weekends I would call up one of the young women I had dated in high school, and we would go on the town. My dates were often Irish American girls from Yorkville. Back during their high school years I had observed that my dates embraced a degree of sensual enthusiasm on Friday nights that might not be available to us later in the weekend. On Saturdays they knelt in penitential darkness before their confessors, blushing at his discourses on "purity." The Holy Sacrament of Penance could afflict a New York Saturday evening with spectral flames and hell's bells.

There were things besides sex that Catholic girls went to hell for, but I can't seem to remember what they were. Nearly every young woman with the benefit of a Catholic education must have acquired, along with her knee socks and vaunted penmanship, some of the *fioretti* of Christian modesty, pious tales designed to harness their hearts and minds to chastity. In one of them, a young person of hitherto spotless virtue—call her Mary Margaret—finds herself parking in the front seat of a non-Catholic sex pervert's customized and wired hot rod. Beside her, this heedless, heartless slimeball pants in amorous entreaty, breathing sin itself into her well-scrubbed ear. And then—oh horrible! We see his dirty fingers at her bra snaps, a low maneuver he's picked up somewhere. Her pants, of a rayon whiter than Ben Bulben's snowy slope, are put aside. A terrible penetration! And in the same moment—God's appalling justice! A lightning bolt! A freight train—because the slimeball, lust-crazed, has parked aslant eternity—the hell-bound tracks of the Babylon Express! And are Paolo and Francesca thrust by an oncoming locomotive into the infernal regions with their so briefly savored weight of mortal sin? You bet. By the time I was home from the sea, the same girls, if not married to firemen or actuarial trainees, were in college or nursing school, and less oppressed by perdition.

Sometimes I could use the serviceman's discount cards I had hoarded during my enlistment to get us tickets to Broadway shows. Usually we went for music, sometimes for jazz at the Central Plaza on lower Second Avenue. The Central Plaza had beer by the pitcher and wonderful Dixieland jazz, although the sets were sometimes vitiated by endless requests for "When the Saints Go Marching In." But jazz greats like Red Allen and Conrad Janis were regular performers. The post-speakeasy mobbed-up cafés on Fifty-second Street were still in place. On the other side of things there were Brubeck or Modern Jazz Quartet concerts at Carnegie Hall, and there was Birdland, the Five Spot, or the Village Vanguard.

The sound of the street was different in those days, and so was the sound of New York speech—*poils* and *ersters* and so on. Toity-toid Street. I remember my mother correcting me, as an urchin, for employing the pronoun *yez* of which the singular was *youse*. My mother was often told that she sounded like Mrs. Roosevelt, a diction she had picked up going to St. Bartholomew's Sewing School before the New York Central tracks were paved over to create modern Park Avenue. It was the old-time *dese* and *dose* that informed the carny patter of those mean, sour little men who talked the suckers into Times Square clip joints. They crooned a welcome to the passing parade, and they could likewise tell you good-bye. They all had the same wizened features; they weighed a hundred and ten pounds each including their saps and knuckle dusters, but they could eighty-six tanked football players so they actually bounced. On one occasion I left my money behind and had to leave my date as security against the check. Thank God she was there when I got back; I had half expected to find the place hurriedly repainted, with Patricia on her way to some far-off island. She was really a good sport about it.

I loved my room at the St. George. The bed was made up every day, the bath was down the hall. Brooklyn Heights was quiet and beautiful and in a way I was a returned native, having been born in Brooklyn, although I had never much lived there. I took advantage of being in Brooklyn to look myself up at Borough Hall; sure enough, I had been born at Good Samaritan Hospital on President Street in 1937. However, my mother's name as registered there was not the name I knew her by. For years I had been coming across identity documents, apparently referring to her, but representing the bearer under a variety of names. Passports, visas, bar bills in Tokyo, even the deed to two cemetery plots in two different cemeteries. The documents were signed in her handwriting affirming two different names. She never got to either of them.

My mother was a puzzle to me. It was not that I never raised the subject of these confusions. But Mom seemed so *confronted,* so pained by my discoveries, that I couldn't bear to embarrass her. Finally I got her drunk and coaxed a few explanations from her, although I'm not sure which versions to believe.

She was disappointed, too, that I had turned out to be nothing but a sailor. Regardless of what the sobby voice-overs proclaim to banners and God-shots on the tube, experts recognize military service as one sign of social dysfunction. My mother actually explained this to me, although not in so many words. I might have countered that not knowing your mother's real name surely indicates a degree of social pathology. Not knowing your father's real name was common enough where I came from. But could not a mother's concealing her identity from her only son (I think) be not uncharitably interpreted as rejection?

In fact, she was very affectionate, and neither rejected me nor slapped me around. When crossed, my mother invoked two fantasies for me to consider, which I did at various times throughout my childhood and later. One was that I would wake up one morning and find her gone—gone, vanished into thin air, never to be found. The other, which bothered me less, was that some dismal morning would find me with my head severed from my body; some mothers were capable of such things, and I might do well to imagine that she might be one of them.

Gladys Grant was how I knew her, the daughter of a tugboat's chief of Scots descent. She remembered passing under the newly constructed Brooklyn Bridge from her father's boat. She lived on Park Avenue next to the railroad tracks and went to St. Bartholomew's Sewing School. She spoke with a cultivated New York accent, and for the first few minutes she could seem more than presentable.

As far as the outside world went, appearances were against us. Twice, when I was eleven, we got reported to the Society for the Prevention of Cruelty to Children, whose officers demanded that we present ourselves for their okay, cruelty-wise. This organization, as I remember, ran some kind of kiddie jail up in the New York barrio. I got a glimpse of it on the way up to their office, about the time I noticed my mother was wearing mismatching shoes. It looked like hard time in there. When we left, I thought some kind of uncruelty dogcatcher would be coming by our place with the wagon. I guess my mother thought so too because we disappeared to Chicago until the school term, when we moved to a different furnished room, and I returned to the daily custody of the Marist Brothers, from whose discipline the Society for the Prevention of Cruelty et cetera offered no recourse.

When the summer of 1958 was over, I managed to swing a job at the *New York Daily News* I had been angling for since my discharge. At the same time I started classes at NYU. Before many weeks were out I knew that college had not been a particularly good idea.

One payday afternoon I was lounging around the St. George Hotel pool preparatory to my evening on the town when the pool lifeguard greeted me by name. I recognized the guard as a high school acquaintance—a big good-looking kid who had been a basketball star, a youth possessed of considerable physical grace and extrovert charm. We both had done our military time and were finding our way through the real world. He was studying acting at the Uta Hagen–Herbert Berghof studios and suggested that I try out myself.

Today, as I try to recall the state of my ambitions at that time, I draw something of a blank. During my time in the Navy I had amassed a small collection of magazine rejection slips, so I know I had some dreams of turning myself into a writer. One of the rejection slips was my proudest possession at that time. It was the form demurrer sent out to disappointed contributors to *The New Yorker,* as elegantly worded as anything the magazine published at that time. What made that familiar totem of obscurity an artifact of such sweet promise to me was the fact that some unknown hand had inscribed a three-word message in one corner of the standard slip: "Try us again." That brief extra message would serve me as an anthem for many years to come.

So the sum of my trophies after a couple of months as a reenfranchised civilian consisted of one treasured rejection slip—something to show my mother, anyway—and a portfolio of writing samples. Beyond this, I incubated a few other half-formulated hopes and dreams and one of them, not surprisingly for a young man of literary aspirations who had grown up around the streets where Lincoln Center would one day rise, had to do with the theater. It seemed to me then that the New York theater—on or off Broadway—was about the most exciting and magical entity in the culture.

I had actually thought a little about acting, and after the conversation with my old classmate I began to imagine a providence at work. Compared to the rocks, the shoals, the silent storms I knew were out there in the endless progression of empty rooms that were the writer's inheritance, a life of performance seemed very attractive.

I was impatient, too, anxious to make something happen. My shuttle between NYU and the *Daily News* had the rhythm of a treadmill. And I reasoned that the study of acting might provide me some insights useful to a dramatist, an ambition that was one aspect of my writerly impulse and one that, even now, I have still not completely despaired of. I did go around to the Hagen-Berghof studios a few times. A number of the students I saw there had brilliant futures before them—Sandy Dennis, if I'm not mistaken, worked at HB around the time I went by.

The urge toward performance, an urge to risk winning the love of an audience or face its scorn then and there, had much to recommend it, compared to the solitary struggle to believe in the power of what I could summon from my own silence. Somewhat later it would bring me to what, for a few tormented hours, looked like another fork in the road.

THREE

When I remember the *New York Daily News* as it was when I went to work there, the first images that come to me are comic strips that ran in color with the Sunday paper. *Dick Tracy* was one. I should hope we all remember Dick with his right-angled jaw, yellow fedora, and two-way wrist radio, the senior detective of a strange city where the cops wore puttees well into the nineteen fifties. The colorful police force stood locked in dubious battle with bands of grotesque criminal mutants. Detective Tracy was hard but fair. Perhaps the tragedy of his own brutally geometric features gave him some insight into the desperate rebellion of deformed local outlaws.

God knows, life must have been martyrdom for Flattop (named for the contour of his head, not his choice of hairstyles) or for Poet, who suffered from a neurological compulsion to sum up his situation in rhyming doggerel ("Such is Life when you meet jerks / He put a bullet through my works!"). Sadder still was the lot of Poet's boss Flyface, whose face, to put it bluntly, drew flies.

Today, cops and robbers are not usually portrayed in comic strips. Amid the prevailing post-irony, melodrama is passé. In the nineteen fifties the funnies had a lot of crime and punishment. The triumph of justice and the comeuppance of the villains usually came in the full-page color Sunday supplements. *Little Orphan Annie* was another feature that served the spirit of America's Most Popular Newspaper. *Orphan Annie* appealed to me for a number of reasons. Its heroine was a sardonic, rather asexual, but identifiably female adolescent. Her expressionist appearance, her orange Afro and picaresque adventures, and especially the cast of characters with whom she matched wits, belonged not to the fifties but to the feverishly imaginative, inappropriately grotesque, comix dreamworld of the twenties.

She was an orphan, an institutional child like me, in flight from the control of a pigeon-breasted, demonic orphanage keeper who wanted her back in custody for reasons that were ever unclear. Mrs. Bleedingheart was her name, and I think she represented New Deal collectivism at its most rapacious. Annie's allies were among the most sinister right-wing activists this side of a Colombian militia. They included Daddy Warbucks, who wore a diamond stickpin and a homburg and seemed to be a mad avuncular pro bono weapons magnate. Daddy employed two deadly murderers as his sinister foreign assistants. One was Punjab, who seemed to be a turbaned Sikh about eight and a half feet tall. The other was a vaguely East Asian, silent man in servant's livery, the Asp.

As Annie's chief ally, Daddy Warbucks would dispatch Punjab and the Asp to eliminate Annie's enemies, feeding them to giant catfish for example while they (enemies) grinned in terror and clasped their hands in vain prayer. At age eleven I would have been glad to ask Punjab and the Asp to visit with the Society for the Prevention of Cruelty to Children, which I imagined to be presided over by Mrs. Bleedingheart. *Little Orphan Annie* killed off as many malefactors as *Dick Tracy*.

It always seemed to me that the attitude that informed these savagely retributive comic strips reflected an attitude at the heart of the parent newspaper. Its headlines rejoiced in patriotic gore, hero cops delivering babies, death in the hotseat.

MARINES MASH CONG IN MUD declared one headline, typed one imagines with clawed fingers and clenched teeth. It succeeded in linking guerrillas with gorillas, pop monsters resisting the American Century, the vision of a slavering ape brought to bay in the jungle swamps of Asia by John Wayne & Co.

The spirit of editorial at the nineteen fifties *Daily News* was that of *The Front Page* and of all the lesser newspaper B movies of the period. These newspaper movies, for all their stock characters, had more zip than many film noirs, newspapers being after all something many movie writers knew a little about.

The editorial department at the *News* was based on its city room. Rewrite men sat at their typewriters at desks arranged in rows of six. Under the system of that time, newspaper stories were a two-person operation. The reporters, whose names came first in the bylines, were out on the street or in the pressroom at Centre Street, New York's Boss Tweed–era basilica of a police headquarters, or in some tenement hallway harassing the grieving mother of a newly electrocuted bandit. Star crime reporters, especially, were often rumored to be functional illiterates or mere neighborhood thugs who happened to have been at reform school with important successful mafiosi. They were portrayed in the movies as holding telephones in the crook of neck and chin and barking, "Sweetheart, get me rewrite!"

Rewrite men, who got second place in the bylines, worked within sight of the city editor. Their desk drawers were usually empty except for a reverse telephone directory, false credentials of various sorts for the reporters, and a bottle of Gold Leaf cognac. Rewrite men on the *Daily News,* men doing follow-up on a story, were instructed to assume out-of-town accents and claim they represented the *Times.* This was intended to disarm socialites who had fallen victim to jewel thieves, or otherwise supposedly respectable citizens who might not choose to have their names appear in the *Daily News*.

The city editors' desks stood out in front of the rewrite men's like the stations of staff officers at the head of a regiment standing inspection. At one end of the big room, beside the rewrite men, a priesthood of elderly sages sat at a slightly depressed baize-topped table rather like a small craps table. The elders were equipped with tomes for their reference, everything from a Bible concordance to Shakespeare's comedies to *Bartlett's* to the *Field Guide to the Insects and Spiders of Greater New York.* At least two of the old-timers at the copy desk would be wearing green eyeshades. Pinned to a billboard at the chief copy editor's head was the yellowing proof of an ancient headline that bespoke a wholesale dismissal of copy editors long ago. PENIS MIGHTIER THAN SWORD, it read.

The One Star went to the trucks about eight o'clock, after some of the Wall Street trading numbers had been checked, and most important of all the final figures of the pari-mutuel handle at Aqueduct racetrack. The Wall Street numbers were winners in various local marginal wagers, but the pari-mutuel handle was the Number—the big Policy winner for just about the whole eastern seaboard. Great care was taken by those responsible not to disappoint through careless error.

Along corridors off the main editorial rooms, in cubicles considerably larger than Dilbert's is today, the feature editors and the staff worked. Sports was the size of the rest of editorial. There were, yes, Society, Theater, Movies, the Women's Page. An English tabloid rented space in one corner staffed by three Britons whose native dress and classic features drew attention. There was a very, very tall Liverpool Irish lady with a milkmaid's complexion and disgraceful teeth who always wore red. Her legs were good and her seams straight; she had the broad hips and wasp waist of a Gibson Girl, while the rest of her towered off and disappeared into the overhead lights. A red-faced man in a checkered shirt read the wire copy with a magnifying glass. A second man confounded us by rolling his own cigarettes from a Prince Albert can.

The *News* when I worked there did not seem to be an equal-opportunity employer. Other newspapers, even in 1958, had multiracial staffs—or at least employed a few members of minorities. I realized this when I went over to the *Herald Tribune*'s city room to pick up some *Tribs* during a strike of New York truckers and mailers. The editorial department of the *Herald Tribune* had employees of every shade. Back at the *News* apartheid was in place, as rigorously present as I had seen it back in Amanzimtoti, Natal, South Africa. Even the sweepers at the *News* were white men, gaunt, sideburned youths from southern Appalachia who were called by names unfamiliar on Forty-second Street, such as Earl and Roy. The cleaning ladies were straight from Warsaw. The *News*'s single employee of any African background was an elderly die maker who ran a little coffee concession on the side. He was a European, however, with an almost impenetrable Scots accent.

The politics and social perspective of the *Daily News* were what America calls "conservative." This meant promoting American capitalism, the most radical transforming power in the history of the world. Familiar social arrangements and structures crumble. The mass of people find themselves dislocated, alienated, and disenfranchised in its wake.

It was the role of papers like the *News* to nurse and manipulate popular prejudice in its own language and discover sources for the referred pains "progress" caused, sources safely distant from any suggestion of economic injustice. Yet class resentment was too valuable a weapon of the dominant corporate interests to dispense with; they wanted it exploited and intensified, yet separated from the notion that corporate America and its workers could have any conflict of interest.

Not that the "conservative" popular press was meant to calm suspicion and discontent. On the contrary. Threats were to be detected everywhere—in reefer madness, in immigrants, above all in ameliorative schemes that threatened economic elites. These had to be seen as foreign-inspired swindles and worse. And the opponents of the status quo had to be identified as "phonies," do-gooders trying to be smarter than everybody else, professors who'd never made a payroll. "People," as one editor used to say at the *Daily News,* "educated beyond their intelligence." Such people tried to make themselves look clever by contradicting the teachings of revealed religion, laughing at authority and deriding the boss, encouraging blacks to get above themselves, fostering disrespect for the police. That is pretty much where we were at the *Daily News,* at the end of the linotype era, the beginning of the end of the newspaper era.

The cartoonist C. D. Batchelor, a colorful figure who presumably was old enough and had been around long enough to get away with wearing a cape and carrying a silver-headed cane, served as a kind of mystic seer for the *News* ideology. His weird, sibylic cartoons provided a somber iconography for the *News*'s opinions. They were ultrapatriotic, saber rattling in a fatalistic way, rather apocalyptic, and certainly without humor.

On the national scene, the editors had no problem with southern racial segregation. Their support for Eisenhower was tepid; Joe McCarthy had been their man. Adlai Stevenson and Hubert Humphrey were eggheads, referred to insultingly. The *News* particularly hated Fidel Castro. During his first official visit to New York I was dispatched with a bunch of photographers to the Waldorf-Astoria. The *barbudos* occupied a floor, Castro and his familiar henchmen before the first purge and a number of attractive young women in much makeup who seemed to be having too much fun to be entirely political. One of the photographers, a guy I used to work with at the wrestling matches, sent me up to one bearded official by Fidel's side.

"Ask him who the girls are," he ordered me.

So I did. The guy gave me a long, contemptuous look.

"They are members of the Twenty-sixth of July Movement," he said haughtily.

Women at the *Daily News* were as yet the distant shadow of an issue. There *were* women there, which is saying something. I'll never forget one exasperated lady in rewrite explaining to the parochial-school graduates on the copy boys' desk the literal and metaphoric significance of the Yiddish word *schmuck.*

Surely anyone over the age of fifty who ever so much as delivered a newspaper has heard the old crack, attributed to H. L. Mencken, about newspaperwomen looking like "British tramp steamers cleaned up for the Queen's birthday." At the *Daily News* it got repeated at least once a month on every shift. The society editor, who bore a pseudo-aristocratic nom de plume that should have belonged to a Colonial Dame, was not one. She was, however, a legendary dame, having forged her own claim on the elite status by getting into the death house to witness the execution of the late Ruth Snyder. Ruth, in her day, was a not unattractive killer-adulteress on whom the Barbara Stanwyck character in *Double Indemnity* was supposedly based. Our society editor-to-be entered in the garb of a nurse.

It should be recorded that the photograph of Ruth Snyder at the moment of impact was taken by another immortal, Hyman Rothman, who, costumed as a doctor (perhaps a short, cigar-smoking doctor) and assisted by the future Miss Society, smuggled a camera into Sing Sing.

Ruth Snyder's death was the occasion of much ongoing hilarity at the *News,* where she survived as "the Babe in the Hot Seat." All women were "babes" at the *News*—witnesses, victims, perpetrators, and colleagues. And, as with what was then called the Homicide Squad, no wrongful death was beyond the purchase of institutional humor.

I remember listening one night to an exchange between Hy Rothman, cruising Central Park in a radio car, and the photo desk. A guy, the police informed the *News,* had done a Dutch off a tree. That is, some lost soul had hanged himself from a tree in the park.

The etymology was interesting. Hanging oneself was known to the police as a "Dutch Act." The name came from the dialect comedians of vaudeville who did immigrant humor, which included rendering German accents. German immigrants in New York in the nineteenth century were often referred to as Dutchmen. The famous Weber and Fields were a Dutch Act. Why should German immigrants be associated with this technique of terminal despair? Some say because nineteenth-century Germans arriving in New York, confronted with the horror they had rashly chosen, ended it all with a rope. Hy was in search of the man who had done the Dutch, but the police report was imprecise as to location.

"What am I supposed to do?" Hyman asked. "Drive around the park looking for a guy hanging from a tree?"

The police culture and that of the *Daily News* were closely entwined.

The editors on the *News* included some eccentric and cultivated characters. But as yellow journalists of the period, they were serving an icon of their own creation. They were, or pretended to be, practitioners of right-wing populism. Their ideal imagined reader was a bigoted, tiny-minded, gum-chewing lout. Thus they became the slaves of their own golem. In the future of the century some version of this proletarian monster would reappear whenever class hatred needed to be dislocated from economics and drafted into service as a confusion.

Downstairs, the Forty-second Street lobby had been transformed into a sunken exhibition hall where a giant globe representing the planet rotated furiously for the crowds passing in or out. The symbols of overheated populism were rampant. The room, lit to a cinematic semidarkness, a cross between a spaceship's bridge and the reptile house at the Bronx Zoo, was an exercise in fascist art deco that outdid anything in Rome or Berlin. Metal silhouettes of a mob *en avant* marched along the wall. Over the decorations was a figure of Lincoln and a supposed quotation.

"God must love the common people," Lincoln is pictured as saying, "he made so many of them."

Frankly, this blood-chilling celebration of American populism, the bonding spirit that informed so many lynchings in the good old days, was a joke to us. Not that there was much we could do about it. What we did was to look for jobs with less morally demeaning publications. These often paid better than the *News* and were far more prestigious. Unfortunately, they usually required more distinguished professional credentials, more extensive education and training, than many of us offered. We had not much leisure to pick and choose. We lived from paycheck to paycheck, plus or minus results from the trotting races at Yonkers Raceway. For our convenience a bookie was located on the composing-room floor. When he retired he "sold" his handbook to some mark, a man not employed by the paper. The man arrived and stood around watching the proofs as they were spiked, waiting for customers. The foreman had to break the news to him; he could trade his handbook for the Brooklyn Bridge.

One thing that kept us going, other than youth and irony, was that we saw changes taking shape in the great world beyond the purview of the *Daily News*.

FOUR

My normal shift on the *News* ended at one in the morning. By rare coincidence, the shift of a classmate of mine also ended an hour after midnight. Janice worked as a guidette at the RCA Building, and sometimes as a seller of tickets to the celebrated Rainbow Room in that building, according to the evening's roster of assignments. She was in Mack Rosenthal's narrative-writing class, as was I, so three times a week our working and school hours more or less coincided.

At the designated hour, Janice would change out of her quasi-military *Star Trek* uniform, put on her black stockings, and braid her ponytail. She had another job as a waitress at the Seven Arts Gallery Coffee Shop on Ninth Avenue and Forty-third Street. I would go along just to watch her bring the coffee, one among a coterie of gang kids, *poètes maudits,* and Times Square characters who sat around paying court to her. The proprietor of the café, an ursine beatnik, was particularly annoyed by my cheap suits, these being, like clean-shavenness, a requirement for employment at the *News*.

My rash attempt to cultivate a set of dapper chin whiskers having nearly subjected me to dismissal, I hardly dared more extravagant affectations. This rendered me subject to his jeering. "Guys in suits don't get the girl, man," he would point out to me from time to time. The girl in question was my classmate Janice; my attentions to her aroused his jealous attraction and his denigration of my low-grade bourgeois wardrobe. This tempted me to observe for his benefit that Wallace Stevens hadn't needed a grinding organ or a monkey with a tin cup to be a poet.

Jack Kerouac read at the Seven Arts, along with Allen Ginsberg, Gregory Corso, Ray Bremser, Ted Joans, and other notables of the Beat era. Eventually I started reading the poetry I'd written at an empty dayside typewriter in the newsroom, working as long as I could get away with it. Janice worked at several of the Village espressos as well, including the long-lived Figaro. We discovered a place on East Sixth Street where the proprietor, a follower of Ayn Rand, sold peyote cactus, an indigenous hallucinogen. Peyote tasted wretched but it provided a glimpse of wonders beyond description. I say a glimpse because it was not until a few years later that I rashly blundered into peyote's kingdom for a closer look.

Later, in the seventies, everything changed. The white-shirted, Mass-attending copy boys were, with some exceptions, no longer exemplars. Black people, women, all sorts of people appeared on the payroll. To be unhip was no longer so cool. There was much wavering then in the ranks of the culture war, and the *News,* as daily newspapers toppled around it, was waiting for a winner.

As it turned out, however, even guys in cheap suits did from time to time get the girl. While Janice's father nervously paced the church nave, a suitably hip clergyman arrived (he was, I believe, a kind of chaplain to the jazz community), and the two of us were married. We soon quit our several jobs and set out for New Orleans like Manon and Des Grieux, New Orleans being the most exotic but affordable destination the Greyhound Corporation afforded romantic newlyweds.

FIVE

Janice and I arrived in New Orleans in 1960 shortly before Mardi Gras. We found an apartment in the French Quarter on St. Philip Street between Bourbon and Royal. The apartment was cheap and functional. We thought it looked like the place where Elia Kazan had located Stanley and Stella in the film version of *Streetcar,* with an interior patio and a balcony over the street. The proprietor of one of the French Market stalls on Decatur Street gave us a striped kitten.

On Friday and Saturday there were a lot of fights on the street. Saturday night lasted from dusk until dawn, when bars closed for an hour to sweep. Every once in a while you could hear a pistol discharged, and see the welter of blue police lights reflected on stucco walls down the street.

A. J. Liebling at that time described New Orleans as a cross between Paterson, New Jersey, and Port-au-Prince, combining as always exquisite observation with a rich imagination. Still the most self-referential city in the country, New Orleans sat at the far end of the post-Faulknerian small-town Deep South, by which I mean the far end from me. It did not really represent the surrounding region, which nevertheless separated it from the rest of urban America.

An immigrant entrepôt, a seaport, a city with a strong Latin and Catholic fabric, New Orleans never seemed totally alien to me. Its accent had elements of Brooklyn speech. The city and its people seemed deeply urban, more like Boston or Philadelphia in some ways than like Atlanta or Dallas. Those latter places were bigger but in those days they were very much a part of the southern Calvinist society around them.

At the same time, New Orleans never imagined itself as other than southern. Its relatively tolerant ways and the presence of a black and mixed-race cultural tradition had earned it the nickname of "Big Easy." As statutorily race-minded as the rest of the South, it managed somehow to seem less ornery about it, at least to outsiders. When J. and I arrived, just a few years after *Brown v. Board,* southern identity was still strong, but its moral self-confidence was reacting to a national repudiation of what the politicians called its "way of life." The South of course was famous for its politicians. Like contemporary pols leading the struggle for values et cetera, the southern politicians knew there was no cause like a lost cause to keep the discontented voters in a state of offended outrage. "Big Easy" or whatever, New Orleans was a tough city for Yankees to find jobs in.

It was also basically a poor one, especially dependent on the oil industry's fortunes.

The demonstrations against segregation had started in North Carolina in 1960, but when we settled in just before Lent of that year things had a long way to go. The Mardi Gras celebrations which I had sort of dreaded were disarmingly cheerful and sweet, observed by both whites and blacks. We were surprised at the number and extent of racially mixed neighborhoods. At the time I thought New Orleans was as residentially integrated as any city I had seen. What most surprised me were the two-story buildings of the public housing projects, many of which consisted of twenty apartments, ten up, ten down. These buildings were segregated in that their tenants alternated white-black-white-black. I had never seen people of different races, poor people at that, living in such proximity. This of course would go. In the seventies New Orleans witnessed the most thoroughgoing white flight anywhere in the country, creating the modest suburbs that sent the Klansman David Duke to the statehouse.

The first jobs I found were two temporary gigs on local assembly lines. Up until then I had missed out on the mass-production experience in America. First at an instant-coffee plant and then at a local liquid-soap factory, I became acquainted with labor discipline as practiced in midcentury. In both places, people got fired as the day lengthened. The irrepressibly social went first, for talking on the line. At mezzanine level, a railed catwalk led to a small glass booth in which two observers watched the line below. One faced left, the other right. Every time one of the temporaries or new hires was dismissed, the speed of the assembly line would slow slightly and then gradually speed up. It was impossible in these circumstances not to feel a trifle jerked around, if not totally dehumanized. Sometimes there was what seemed to be an arbitrary speedup, announced by the sounding of a siren. There was half an hour for lunch plus a break in midmorning and another in midafternoon. Breaks consisted of ten minutes at a plywood table in a green-and-yellow room, mainly to let people have a smoke, forbidden on the line. The break room was also equipped with coin machines that contained things that could be swallowed.

After being banished by the Janus-faced pairing in the booth, I found the second assembly-line job under circumstances essentially identical. My dismissal, by an undead foreman, was less polite. The cashier presented me with a pink slip and a work schedule for the following week. My schedule said: "Terminated." There were boxes as on a speeding ticket and two were neatly checked in. One check keyed the word "Attitude." The other indicated "No incident of theft of material property or cash prior to termination." Since the last line on the document told me I might submit the thing to prospective future employers, I understood that it was a qualified recommendation.

"I never said a word to anybody," I told the cashier.

"Y'all come back," the cashier said.

Waiting for the bus downtown, I thought vengefully about the bright future when the unions would arrive to organize the plant. Time would change things and would bring all kinds of social justice to America, North and South. It felt "inevitable." In those days the word had connotations beyond death, famine, pestilence, and war.

I passed through a number of off-the-books, cash-only positions. The next recorded employment I found was in the service of *Collier's Encyclopedias*, a set of thick, handsomely bound volumes I suppose was as useful as any other. Each morning the *Collier's* chief salesperson picked us up at a designated meet and drove us to one of the towns within an hour or two of New Orleans. A town in St. Tammany or Washington Parish would be likely, Covington or Bogalusa, or we might work across the state line in Pearl River County, Mississippi. There were difficulties. Many of the towns had ordinances that outlawed door-to-door selling. Voter-registration drives were in action all over the South. In many towns northern volunteers had come to the deepest South for the first time, assisting local initiatives that were sometimes creating an African American constituency where none had existed since Reconstruction.

I was there and I did nothing to help. I have always liked to believe—I do believe—that my first novel, A Hall of Mirrors, was a modest shot from the right side. It was literally the best I could do though it didn't require the heroism of a Viola Liuzzo or a Mickey Schwerner. Ironically, the self-serving career that led me to it landed me, though very, very briefly, in jail.

One night just after sunset we were working the poorer white quarter of a burg on the Mississippi side. By then I had found that the Mississippi Gulf Coast had some things in common with New Orleans. Most obvious was a degree of ethnic diversity that eased the pressure of what W. J. Cash called the "proto-Dorian bond," the obsessive pursuit of white supremacy as a form of religion that tormented the dreams and threatened the lives of so many. The Greeks of Pass Christian, the Croatians of Biloxi, had inherited a few ethnic concerns that went back beyond institutionalized memories of the Confederacy. But the Mississippi town we were selling in that evening was not on the coast; it was far enough north in the state for the sultry wind to carry the scent of pine and tupelo and to encounter mule-drawn wagons on the shoulder of the dirt roads. The town had been famous for the rough turp camps where Huddie Ledbetter had worked between jolts, and it contained the headquarters of an international logging company that took longleaf pine. The land was flat but there were sizable Indian mounds around town, some with houses built over them, approachable by wooden steps.

The *Collier's* pitch was to be memorized and seemed unchanging as the canon of the Mass. Twenty-five years later, visiting in a Houston suburb, I watched a youth the age I had been recite the same incantations. These, being interpreted, went more or less like this: "Good evening, sir" (and you look the good ole boy straight in the eye; if he's not home, move on, you don't pitch Mama): "Lucky sir! Your ideal household has been selected for a marketing experiment which will afford you big savings. We propose to place a set of encyclopedias in your home. You may not know this but your neighbors look up to you and model their lives on yours. If you take in our encyclopedias at an absurdly low price your neighbors will see and— you know how it is? When the right people have got something fine everybody else wants it too, am I right?" (Here exchange knowing looks and melancholy smiles at the simplicity and pathetic predictability of human nature. If no reaction is forthcoming on his part, give him the look and the smile.) "Only thing is, heh heh" (invitation to join in cynical laughter) "they'll be paying five hundred times what you done paid with your extended EZ payment discount price. Sound good to you? The kids will bless you for it. They'll excel, yessir!" And et cetera.

First door I hit was opened by a sharp-eyed man with a little brush mustache. Was that a gun in his hand? Yes, it was, by God. Some kind of revolver. He put it back in a shaving kit he was holding. At some point in the pitch I asked, jovially, if the revolver was loaded.

He looked at me in mild disgust. "Gun wouldn't do you no good wasn't loaded, now would it?"

"Ha ha," I replied. (A good jest, Montressor.)

At one point he offered me what he called a coldrink. I accepted. He went back into the kitchen and I heard him preparing it. He spoke to someone. I heard a child's voice, the child whose future would shine with the wisdom of Daddy's Yankee encyclopedia.

"You get to goddamn hell something something!" shouted ole Dad, quite angrily.

The man told me he was a long-distance bus driver. He said he drove eighteen-wheelers too but I didn't believe that part. He began to ask me depressingly dumb questions. He asked me if there was anything in the encyclopedia about evolution or the mixing of the races. I assured him there wasn't. It wasn't my finest hour. I was desperate for a paycheck. He signed up. He seemed a little angry.

We walked outside and he turned on his front door light. His house was on top of one of the Indian mounds with wooden steps leading up to the door.

"You say you sure nothin' in it about evolution or the mixing of the races?"

"That's right," I said. He had signed the goddamn thing. I was heartily tired of my own song and dance.

"Better not be."

A million gnats, moths, and mosquitoes spun around the lighted tin carriage lamp beside his front door. One after another little insects singed their wings against its flyspecked glass casing and fell into the ruined spiderweb at its base. The light was dazzling me. But when I turned away there was still light in my eyes. The wooden steps were steep and the rail beside them was flimsy. I had my hand in front of my face and I realized that there was light in front of me and below. Someone was shining a power torch beam into my eyes. A voice heard only in dreams (or bad movies) said, "Come down them steps real slow."

It was the sheriff. Through the shafts of light I could make out the star-shaped badge on his work shirt. He had a Stetson and stitched cowboy boots; he was leaning one foot forward on the wooden steps. He had a gut over his gun belt and a holstered pistol. I was being arrested.

They rounded up the whole team, which included quite a few non-southerners, and took us to jail. There we remained until a local lawyer was retained by *Collier's* to spring us. Over coffee with the deputies we learned that the Yankee inflections were what had brought the sheriff. Townfolk, including the eighteen-wheeler jock wannabe, were afraid that history had come for them in the form of outside agitators. Not quite, but it was coming.

A couple of weeks after I was liberated from my Mississippi imprisonment I saw a strange sign on the wall of a Royal Street coffee shop. It was printed in a kind of liturgical script with a cross and what looked like upraised spears. The largest drawn figure was of a metal chalice, and the title of the production was *The Cup*. There was what appeared to be a photograph of Jesus Christ in the middle of the sign. Closer inspection revealed it to be the photo of an actor in costume, a melancholy long-faced man with an actorish name who according to the sign portrayed "the Christus." The sign was soliciting apprentice actors for roles in a traveling Passion play, which the sign said was "North America's most reverent and moving commemoration of Our Lord's sacrifice." It seemed to move from town to town, sponsored by local churches. I wrote the telephone number down, along with the particulars of the next few performances.

I didn't know what was on my mind; at seventy-five cents and a dollar fifty, the tickets were in excess of our entertainment budget. At that time we were surviving through our discovery of an old New Orleans amenity, the friendly beanery waitress. The friendly beanery waitress could slip you a slice of white bread and redeye gravy to keep you whole until the next opportunity came to borrow a quarter. Public assistance was not available.

I mentioned the odd joint to Janice, who politely told me she didn't think she'd like to go. Then I called the number of the operation and pretended to be an applicant for a role in the reverent commemoration. Anyway, I thought of myself as pretending.

The show's local operation was in a small suite of rooms at a shabby, barely respectable hotel on Canal Street. The hall door was opened by a tall, slender woman with long silky hair. She had the unsound blue eyes of an Ibsen leading lady magnified by wire-framed glasses. Gorgeous was the word for her. Hers had been the voice that responded to my telephone call. I later learned that she was one of the Christus's two lovely daughters. In fact, I never got to see the other one, but of her comeliness I have no doubt. The sisters had various clerical and organizational duties with the group. They also performed onstage, bits like Pilate's wife and the serving girl who denounces Peter.

The man himself, the Christus, was pale and fine featured, with a high forehead and a bald dome. The fringe around his skull made him look tonsured. He wore very darkly colored aviator sunglasses and a black lightweight suit. His voice was cultivated and, inevitably, somewhat affected. His name, as I had noticed, was unlikely and resonant. All at once I recognized it as the name of a radio actor on one or another of the radio dramas I'd listened to.

"Attitude," he told me, "is the key. People feel as though they're at a church service. They're open and worshipful. Sensitive. They may not identify a bad attitude but they are aware of it. Something will trouble them."

I nodded thoughtfully. Was attitude catching up with me again? As a youth, I was as innocently bad attituded as I could get away with.

"You cannot disdain the story. You cannot disdain your character. Of course you can't despise the audience."

The audience, he told me, would consist of small-town folks all over North America, and the outfit was called the International Gospel Theatre (*sic*). It worked its way like a wheat-harvesting combine, rolling up from the Texas plains to the edge of the muskeg in northern Manitoba.

The character I would compete to portray was the Chief Temple Guard, although I would have to learn several parts. As CTG I would command a corps of teenage Bible school students, always locally recruited, who would serve as Herodian spear carriers. It was also the Guards' responsibility to put up and break the sets under the supervision of their Chief.

The audiences, the Christus informed me, were unlikely to have seen a live show before unless it was perhaps a previous year's performance by the International Gospel Theatre. He said his group had been offered good money to perform on tape. But the Christus believed in live performance. It was the only way to bring out the sacramental quality of a Passion play. Did I grasp this? I said I did but he told me anyway, about the Thirty Years' War and the plague and the burghers of Oberammergau. I had always mixed up the town with the half-timbered village that hired the Pied Piper. He had me do some readings from the King James Bible. Job and Ecclesiastes. Revelation. I asked him if I would have to read such stuff on the road. He said he liked my readings. He said from time to time we would open the show with a little scripture.

I saw the comely daughter who took phone calls looking at me. She had listened to me wailing on the Seven Seals and the Beast from the Sea and so on. The Christus noticed me returning her look.

"You have folks?" he asked. "Married?"

"No," I heard myself say. "Not me."

"Yeah, well," he said, "it's no spot for a family man."

The last thing I could endure to be at that moment was a family man.

The Christus said he thought well of my work and might decide to hire me. He had a few other men to hear. For some it was just a courtesy; they were past it.

"So you want to play Chief of Temple Guards!" he said. He had the kind of smile called vulpine. In his pictures with a Jesus wig, he looked like Rasputin. He told me to check back in person at the end of the day. I thought of going home to the Quarter but I didn't want to see J. I was contemplating an unspeakable treachery. Or at least I thought I was. I went to the public library on Federal Square, where it was cool, and read the city histories. There was an entire room filled with genealogy. I settled down in Fiction and read all of *The Plumed Serpent*. I admired Lawrence very much then. From time to time the bottom fell out under my stomach when I remembered what I was contemplating and I said, "Oh, God." Which was enough to turn the other readers in my direction. When the time came, by my cigarette-coupon watch, I replaced the book and went into the glaring heat of downtown.

Back on Magazine Street, the Christus's lovely daughter smiled without looking at me as she let me pass.

"Well," Mr. Christus said solemnly, "you may join us if you choose."

For a second I didn't get it.

When I understood, I said: "Can I bring someone along?"

"You certainly can't."

"Ah," I said. "When will we be back here?"

"I wouldn't think for the best part of a year. If we get any gigs in this state at all. Problem?"

I shook my head, feeling ever fainter. "No problem."

"Can you come with us to Lake Chickasaw?" he asked. "We're there tomorrow night."

"Can you make it?" he said, when I didn't answer. "We'll book you a room in this hotel tonight. You won't even have to share. This time."

"We'll buy you dinner," his young daughter said. "If you can get back here."

"Sure," I said. I felt as though I must be trembling. The thought of their dinner made me ill. I wanted the crazy life I was looking at more than anything. The last trace of gypsy life on the continent. I did not want to be stuck in New Orleans with my pregnant wife.

All at once it seemed that the chance at theater I had opted away from in New York had spun around my way in these absurd trappings, in a mode for which "provincial" would be too pretentious a term. I wanted feverishly to clamber aboard this absurdity, and I wanted the ruthlessness and sangfroid to try. I don't know what I saw shining there. Maybe just the chance to change the life I was making for myself and start a new one. Anyway, my theatrical fantasy was back shimmering, available if I could find the resources to go for it.

I walked back through the hot streets, across Canal and down Royal to St. Philip, through the patio and up the inner stairs. Janice was on the balcony, leaning back on her chair, resting her feet. Naturally slim, she was showing seven months' pregnancy. She looked radiant and lovely, a loose lock of brown hair over her eye.

"Where've you been?" she asked me.

"The library. And pursuing this phantom job."

I wanted a drink. I took a few dollars, which I could ill afford, from our pathetic money stash and went down to the corner saloon.

I had a couple of twofers at the bar and took a jug of plonk home with me.

"What was the phantom job?" she asked. I was sitting a couple of feet away from her, looking down toward the river. I was thinking of towns like Lake Chickasaw, of the whole continent disappearing into times past. There was no chance that an experience like performing in *The Cup* would ever come my way again. I was too young to be tied down in this way. A world of adventures awaited, across continents and across oceans. A world of beautiful and available women of which the Christus's daughter, who indeed seemed to like me, was only the first.

I looked over at Janice. And I thought, She's done it to herself, committed to all this too young; she was just a kid. Committed to a louse like me, she'll find out what a selfish creep I am. She can pass the baby to her parents; they could help her, and she could have a life. And in turn I could have a life and cross those continents and oceans to where life was richer. To embrace fate, to live out the cruel rituals of life at the core of the flame, to do and to see everything. Oh, wow! To have the courage to be brutal and to reject convention and compromise. Chief Temple Guard was only the beginning.

I snuck another look at her, and indeed she looked beautiful. And being so young, she looked innocent and trusting. She looked as though she loved me.

So. At that moment I knew that I was not going anywhere. I loved her and *that* was fate. If I stood up to leave, my legs would fail, my frame wither, my step stumble forever. All my strength was subsumed by this rash, so unwise, too early love. There was no hope, except in this woman. She would give birth, and the new life would assert itself and take over *our* center and prepare to replace us. Instead of far continents it was boring parenthood; we would just roll down the old biology road like every other sucker. Trapped by nature's illusion, like a bug by a predator's coloration.

I felt infinitely relieved, happy for a moment as I would hardly ever be. I thought: This rejoicing shows my mediocrity. Just another daddy Dagwood bourgeois jerk. Because if I had been destiny's man, I thought, I would have walked—strided away with my bus schedule and my backpack, ready to ride from Chickasaw Lake to the Great Slave. But I was not, I could not, not any more than I could fly. I guess I also knew at about that moment that I would never leave her, not ever, that this thing was forever. Your great soul, your world historical figure, would have walked. Not Bob. Not your daddy, children. Leave your mother? No.

So like the original Christus and the young man who could not leave the life he knew, I turned my back on the wager and went my way.

————

The census, which my wife worked until virtually the day before she gave birth, was a dazzle of New Orleans strangeness. If kabbalah angels and Mayan gardens had appeared behind the flaking doors of impoverished New Orleans it would not have surprised us. Moreover we were drawing the best temporary pay in the South as far as we knew.

The hospital in which my daughter was born was Huey Long's gift to his private tinhorn republic. It was segregated, which meant that everything had to be done twice, replicated. Only the poor went there. Fathers were not allowed in maternity. Doctors and nurses were condescending and sarcastic. It seemed that only the black nurse's aides were kind. We had a girl and we called her Deidre.

We moved apartments once, letting some passing friends stay

out the rent on St. Philip Street. Maybe out of some secret unspoken hate, a cruel sense of humor—who knows?—these people left the remains of their shrimp dinner in our sink. It remained there for four days of blistering New Orleans summer. The place had to be fumigated.

One day I was walking down Barracks Street when a black Cadillac pulled up beside me. The passenger door opened. A well-dressed man I did not at first recognize addressed me cheerfully.

"Hey, Stone! Get in."

I got in beside him, and the air-conditioning in his car was very welcome. I saw that it was my landlord, Mr. Ruffino.

"What you do that to me for?" Mr. Ruffino inquired. He was referring to the shrimp in the sink. "I ever do anything like that to you?"

I was surprised and alarmed. Perspiring heavily all at once, air-conditioning or not, I explained what I knew must be the circumstances. Somehow I convinced him.

Maybe Mr. Ruffino took pity on my recent fatherhood. He was later helpful in getting me into the seamen's union. He also revived my aborted show-business career by introducing me to his friend Dominick.

It was the era of poetry readings to jazz, and Dominick fancied the idea of introducing these items at his Dumaine Street bar. I read some of the pieces I'd read in the Seven Arts. Local talent and people driving in from New York or the Coast or Mexico came through. We passed a glass goblet and split the proceeds. Sometimes, after Tulane football games, the players and their followers would come in and throw bananas at us. This cost them nothing, since the bananas, in bunches off the dock, were hung from the ceiling and the bar pillars.

On one occasion Dominick, who was taking increased pleasure in these upscale shows, rented a bunch of avant-garde Yugoslav cartoons to precede the main event. Drunk partisans of the Crimson Tide, which had prevailed over Tulane that day, disrespected the cartoons and threw bananas at the screen. Dominick stepped forward in front of a phalanx of his heavyset, frowning waiters. He put up his hands for quiet.

"Y'all don' wanna tro bananas at the screen," he told the customers decorously. "Don' do it."

The next show was us. We were reading aloud from "John Brown's Body." I don't remember whose idea that was. Not mine. It is, in fact, a most moderate and open-minded poem, although maybe not a great one. Still, it sounded out of place a block or so off the levee.

"Horses of anger . . . ," we read.

The customers began to hoot and jeer. They started throwing bananas again. The well-dressed Tulane alums, the 'Bama dolts, the tourists—all started screaming and throwing bananas. We performers covered up and tried to flee. This only encouraged the mob.

Suddenly we heard a body fall. And then another. "Degenerate cocksuckers!" The very words I had in mind! It was Dominick. His rage at degenerate cocksuckers who failed to appreciate Stephen Vincent Benét was uncontainable. In very little time he and his staff had cleared the place. When the last philistine had been ejected, threatened, and booted in the ass, he shook hands with the readers.

"Y'all was good," he said. "We'll do it another time."

I learned a lot that year in New Orleans. Janice did too. The closer to street level you live, the more you have lessons thrust upon you. One I remember very clearly was an experience I had while taking the U.S. census.

It was hot, as it could be only down there. I knocked on the door of one of the decrepit wooden houses on the edge of downtown, in an area I believe has been demolished for the construction of the Super-dome. If the dome builders didn't get it, no doubt Hurricane Katrina did.

Inside, half a dozen people were gathered around a bed. Beside it, a single candle burned at the feet of a plaster Virgin. Cloth blinds had been drawn over the windows to keep back the killing sun, and the candle was the only source of light in the room. As I advanced toward the bed, I saw that all the people around it had turned to watch me. Looking over their shoulders I saw that, lying there, with clean white sheets drawn almost up to her chin, was a very old woman. Her skin was a café-au-lait color and engraved with fine wrinkles. Her toothless face was like an old turtle's. She breathed with difficulty. She was clearly dying.

I was delighted to learn that the folks in the room were attendant relatives from two different households. This was a tactical coup, census-wise, and a labor-saving stroke of luck. In my brisk impatience to record the statistical details of everyone's life, it took me a moment to realize that these people were strangely unforthcoming. Looking up from my forms, I confronted their eyes. Their eyes were calmly questioning, almost humorous. I stood and stared and returned to my jottings until suddenly it hit me. Someone is dying here. These people have come to attend a death. Perhaps this was not the ideal time for census taking? After this leap of understanding the rest followed unbidden.

That had this been a white middle-class household I would never have been allowed past the door.

That had this been a white middle-class household I would never have dreamed of entering a sickroom, of approaching a deathbed, asking cold irrelevant questions of people who had come to mourn and pray.

That what had happened there was entirely determined by the politics of race and class—how blinding that can be, how dehumanizing, how denying of elemental human dignity and respect. Walking along Dryades Street in the paralyzing glare, the whole wave hit me. The questions I had asked, one after another, that they had endured from me. Place of birth. Estimated year's income. Mother's full name. Condition of residence? We didn't ask that one; the answer was always dilapidated and we checked the appropriate square.

I thought of that afternoon and those people almost twenty years later, when that house was gone, the whole neighborhood vanished, and the Republican convention in progress in the giant arena that had replaced it. I thought of it again when Katrina came and scattered such people, their houses and their graves and their prayers, to the four winds.

Just as the unimaginable summer heat began to subside, we started north. Janice traveled on the train with the baby and the French Market cat. I planned to hitchhike. Rides were so bad through Mississippi that I tried a freight train, the one and only time in my life I've ever done so. The yardmaster at Picayune, Mississippi, was friendly. He advised me not to ride. Then he reminded me to always put a two-by-four in the freight car door to keep it from slamming shut forever. He taught me a little of the number system that keyed the destinations of freight cars. I made it to Birmingham, Alabama, not very far. I was quite happy to get out. Hitching over the mountains, hassled by police, threatened and occasionally befriended, I got to Washington, D.C. It was the day of the first Nixon-Kennedy debate. It was fall, and cool. I headed for the Apple and Janice, wanting nothing so much as to see her again.

When you were young in those days and thought you had exhausted the resources of your hometown and the landscape that had nourished you, you waited for a green light at the intersection of the great American road. When it flashed go, you went.

My bride and I had a problem, native New Yorkers as we were, children of what we never for a moment doubted was the Rome, Athens, and Jerusalem of our postwar world. The problem of course was where, where—since we believed on the assurance of high rollers and Algonquin wits that everywhere outside the Apple was Bridgeport. In fact, I harbored another, a secret conviction: that authenticity, whatever it was, resided somewhere else, somewhere that I was not. I'd know it when I saw it, I had even glimpsed it from afar in my travels, but it seemed to evaporate at my approach. Authenticity was out there beyond the vast fields of the Republic, eluding me, but I believed in it faithfully, a place, a magical coast, a holy mountain where folk of unsullied unself-consciousness labored at genuinely valid occupations and justified the race and the nation, where dwelt the thing itself, the McCoy.

The best and truest thing in *On the Road* is Kerouac's description of his hero's experience of the same longing as he studies the red band of Route 10 winding from Bear Mountain Bridge to Sacramento. Naively Sal sets out to follow it and the real America. For Sal it resides in the person of Dean Moriarty—that is, Neal Cassady. From the West Side I knew authenticity was approachable by way of the bus station in the Hotel Dixie, then under the river and beyond the Palisades, where its lights might be visible on summer nights from Riverside Park. Scott Fitzgerald and young Truman Capote might dream of Manhattan, but that was a dream denied me. The fact that I was there and always had been meant the treasure was buried on a different island.

Drifting through the rich, strange, brutal fever dream that was New Orleans fifty years ago I was astonished to learn some things I hadn't known. As married kids in the middle of the French Quarter, our new baby hidden from the insect hordes under an old prom-night crinoline of Janice's, we found ourselves surviving. Nor was our poverty a game of *la vie bohème;* there were no well-off parents to save our skins, no prospect of refugee status and rescue to call on. I doubt either of us then knew what a trust fund was; we might have guessed it was the value of the quarter you owed someone for your most recent slice of white bread and redeye gravy. The city of New Orleans had not required us, neither us nor our new daughter, born with the grudging assistance of Huey Long's Charity Hospital.

It's so long ago now that I have only fragments of recollection, river mists, magnolia, gardens enclosed in old stone. Also police sirens, and shouts in the street, tambourines and the notes of a clar-inet in the twilight at the end of a blazing day. Recently, the scenes of the city under the fist of Hurricane Katrina brought it all back.

It turned out there is nothing like parenthood and a dose of star-vation to still youth's craving for authenticity. Without intending to, we had placed ourselves in a strange, profoundly self-referential place at a time when history had come to sweep away its revered past. A year there had given me something like a sense of life lived in time, and I began to imagine something like a novel.

SIX

I went back to New York, my head spinning with the things we'd seen and been. The three of us, Janice and I and our New Orleans–born daughter, settled into an apartment on St. Mark's Place, off the Bowery. In those days the northern end of the Lower East Side still bore traces of the old German section that had been called Kleine Deutschland. That neighborhood had been demoralized and destroyed in 1904 by the disaster of the *General Slocum*, an excursion steamer that burned and sank in Hell Gate, taking the lives of over a thousand women and children attending a Lutheran church outing. But the ruins of it were manifest if you knew where to look. Across the street from our window was the old German *Schutzenverein*. Engraved in the lintel of its handsome brick building was the motto *Einigkeit macht stark,* "Strength in union." The German sporting club had become a Polish club. Another Polish social club down the street, the Polski Dom, often jammed on holidays and for Gypsy weddings, would be transformed into the Dom, center of the Andy Warhol universe. The Polish and Ukrainian dimensions of the neighborhood had expanded and would expand more when new waves of immigration arrived. The huge Ukrainian Uniate church of St. George and St. Basil stood on Hall Place, across from McSorley's Ale House. A quarter at McSorley's bought you two steins of the house ale, all that was served. Except for some Cooper Union students it was an old-timers' hangout. It refused service to women, refused it noisily. The bartender, if a woman entered, shouted, "No ladies!" at the top of his voice and rang a deafening ship's bell until the mortified woman left. My sister-in-law staged a one-girl underage guerrilla raid on the place, darting in, grabbing a full stein from in front of a doddery old boy, and draining it while the bartender clanged desperately and went hoarse with shouting. Sister-in-law had a dazzling smile.

The Anderson Theater still gave Yiddish performances, Second Avenue had Ratner's and Rappaport's. There was great bread of every kind and ex-speakeasy restaurants. Variety Photoplays near Fourteenth played westerns in triple-feature mode while mice ran over your feet. Tenth Street east of University Place had the small galleries that thrived through the days of abstract expressionist popularity. On University Place itself was the Cedar Bar, where Franz Kline, de Kooning, and hundreds of memorable characters of lesser note went regularly. Janice and I also.

At the 302, on Ninth Street, was New York's best-known transvestite floor show. The Hell's Angels had opened a headquarters on Sixth Street. "Baron," one of the innumerable types who were known by that name over time, ran his espresso café on Sixth Street as well, and dealt psychedelics ordered from a cactus farm in Texas. W. H. Auden lived in an elegant brownstone at the First Avenue end of St. Mark's. The number of loft parties increased as the fire department eased up on artists occupying lofts. Going to one was like going to a party in the subway. The Bowery then had hundreds of flophouses and roach-challenged bars with pressed-tin walls, where you hoped they used soap to wash the beer glasses. The boiled eggs behind the bar were prewar.

A strange social development was taking place on skid row, something that might have escaped our notice at a different time. The Bowery was undergoing a kind of race war that it would have been absurdly euphemistic to call integration. Black down-and-outers, whose absence few neighborhood whites had noticed before, began appearing at corners and in the doorways of the chicken-wired hotels. In earlier times, the derelict quarters of major cities were segregated. The Bowery occupants were overwhelmingly elderly white men, who ranged in degree of poverty from the scrofulous, dying bundles of rags in the gutter to men in dry-cleaned thirdhand suits and clean shirts who drew some sort of pittance once or twice a month. This small sum they would providently turn over to the owners of the bargain restaurants where they ate or to the hotel keepers at their rooming house. The meal tickets and room chits kept them lodged and fed even if they fell off the wagon. Most, though not all, were alcoholics. There were virtually no women among them.

Who kept up or enforced the racial barriers? Maybe hard cases who ran the beaneries and hotels. Maybe the police, forcing black paupers up to the skid rows in Harlem. But at a certain point around 1960 changes were perceivable. Things being what they were and are, black men faced impoverishment more frequently and at a younger age than most whites. For the same reasons, larger numbers of poor black men had served longer terms in prison. The black newcomers were often younger and less physically ruined than the white derelicts, more used to more serious fighting than at least many of the whites and, perhaps, more involved with drugs. They were also angry; there were men who had been brutalized and whipped, or served on chain gangs and in turp camps.

What began to happen was that the social system recently established in prisons took over the Bowery. On the most productive panhandling corners, and in the homeless shelters, the older white men began to disappear. In a way, it was simply a question of the young, in a desperate situation, displacing the old. It went, I think, unnoticed and unmentioned by the city at large. Older men of all races fled the Bowery and looked for relative safety. But there was no protection for anyone. The Darwinian quality one glimpsed was as shocking as anything I ever saw.

Since getting back to New York, I had found a job with an advertising company that specialized in promotions for furniture. The furniture was of the sort that was sold on time to poor people. There were three grades of it, and its style was contemporary Scandinavian or American Colonial. Copywriters, such as I was, received the ad layouts with the furniture pictured and the spaces for advertising copy indicated. The game was to supply the words of the ad copy; these inevitably were adjectives and adverbs. "Lovely," "Exquisite," and "Handcrafted." The last term remained meaningless to me. It seemed to make a picture, but a picture which I could never quite visualize clearly. Maybe a graceful, disembodied hand fondling the sensuous curves of an imitation-maple chair back. It was pretty boring work. The mind was a monkey. What was most obnoxious about the job was its aftereffect. As a registered loser on every sucker list in New York, I could be sure of receiving my own overwritten, chiseling copy in every weekend mail, pitching myself with my own scam.

I began to write about New Orleans, although I found it extremely difficult to write on weekends and after work. I was afflicted, it seemed, with some kind of pathological laziness. Maybe it was depression. Maybe just bad character. Somehow your worst characteristics stay with you when your good stuff goes.

One winter day Janice and I were walking along Washington Square when we happened to run into our old professor Macha Rosenthal. Mack had conducted the one writing class I attended at NYU before I dropped out of school. Since that class I've thought about this man continually, and there is no one other than Janice to whom I owe more. His class at NYU was the most fun anyone, certainly I, ever had in a classroom. Outside academia, Mack was a fine poet and America's foremost Yeats scholar. In our workshops he was a kind and witty critic, who never lost his wry edge or his sense of humor, and his classes were champagne, especially but not only if he liked your work. I never learned much from teachers in my life, but he was one I learned from.

On the square that night Janice and I, who had met in his class, were back from New Orleans, parents and no longer students. For the second time since I'd met him, Mack mentioned the Wallace Stegner Fellowships at Stanford University. These were, as far as I know, the only writing workshops at that time that offered paid fellowships to writers with no academic credentials. The deal was simply to show up every Wednesday for a workshop and to write. It didn't offer very much money, but if one's spouse worked, life was possible. Mack urged me again to try for it, and this time I did.

A few months later I got the letter: I'd received one of the Stegner Fellowships. The thought of it almost forty-five years later makes my heart quicken. Life is short.

In the late spring Janice, our small daughter, and I took the train west. It was the first we'd ever seen of the Far West, the first of California.

SEVEN

Janice, Deidre, and I arrived in San Francisco late in the spring, just as the cold seasonal weather was closing in (Mark Twain has been quoted as saying that the coldest winter he ever spent was a summer in San Francisco) and the foghorn on Alcatraz sounded the Rock's last year of its operation as a penitentiary.

Our apartment had a Murphy bed, the first one I'd ever seen outside a Laurel and Hardy movie. It was on the fourth floor of a five-story building, on the lowest slope of Russian Hill, a short distance from the bay. Walking up the hill at night, we would fall under the spell of the prison island's foghorn and the searchlight arcs sweeping the veil of mist.

There had been at least one escape attempt while we were in town. A famous local actor was said to have parked a car in the marina, keys in the ignition, a bag of sandwiches on the seat—just in case the cons made it through the currents and dodged the sharks and patrol boats. This kind of gesture defined the city at that time. Halfway up the foggy hill from us was an Italian restaurant, candlelit, with red-checkered tablecloths, fiascoes, even a kindly proprietor who extended credit.

"The City," the *Chronicle*'s columnist unrelentingly called the place, with a jaunty suburban provincialism that provoked your youthful hipper-than-thou. Herb Caen was the sort of columnist who might refer to himself as a "scribe," a "scribe" from "Baghdad on the Bay." My picayune revenge was to call the place "Frisco" at least once a day—call it "Frisco" and watch a moment of well-bred revulsion curl the thin lips of the tweedy, nice-looking people who seemed so large a percentage of the local population in those days. (Around 1960, a New York wit compared the ambience of San Francisco to being "stuck in an elevator in Lincoln Center.") But it was sweet, a pearl necklace of a city, at once exotic and Yankee, restrained yet dazzling, possessed of a beauty that went on surprising. And it was charming, a word I could not then honestly employ, because it described qualities beyond my conscious comprehension. No one had ever used it about New York.

Both Janice and I held down jobs during our summer in San Francisco. I had the day job, in a shirt factory on Mission Street. Janice worked night shift at the Bank of America while I babysat. When Stanford's fall term began in September, we moved out to Menlo Park near the Stanford campus. In the autumn of 1962 (a sunny sea-son I couldn't, newly transplanted to California, quite get myself to call "fall") a number of us set out from Palo Alto to San Francisco in a friend's Volkswagen bus. At the time I was erotically programmed for Volkswagen buses, conducting an affair, deliciously illicit, with a young graduate-student wife who drove one. I remember anticipating the distant sight of that bus as she approached our rendezvous, recognizing her, honey-haired at the wheel, her groceries and toddler secured in the backseat. Illicitness was not going to be around much longer, with its pangs and guilty pleasures. We were about to abolish the very notion.

In the days of illicitness one was serious. One struggled against the pressures of one's early marriage and premature parenthood. One tried to behave like the characters in French New Wave movies—a treacherous phone call, a shrug, a Gauloise. A busload of youthful libertines, most of us in some manner of postgraduate fealty to Stanford, we drove to San Francisco that day on the Bayshore Freeway, Highway 101.

Our objective on the autumn day in question was an evening out, in which it would be possible to catch John Coltrane at the Jazz Gallery and Lenny Bruce at the Hungry i, within half a mile of each other. We had decided to prepare for this embarrassment of riches by ingesting large amounts of peyote, the inoffensive-appearing little cacti which in those days were mainly available south of the border, in Mexican market stalls, offered for sale by tranquilly composed Native American ladies who looked as though they knew something most other people didn't. As we now realize, this was the case.

Certainly they knew more about things than I did, hurtling through sunny California toward the evening's pleasure. I was not completely checked out on what I knew, as opposed to all the rest. Someone had bought a great many gelatin capsules, available from corner drugstores. Someone else had boiled a huge mass of the slime green cactus meat into a loathsome dinosaur-colored ratatouille and jammed it into the capsules. Peyote tasted even more disgusting than it appeared, and one did anything to suppress the taste. All of us, three or four couples, proceeded to swallow a handful of these things, an average of six or so each. I admitted to six; in fact I had taken twelve. Secretly, I was convinced I knew the score. I had taken peyote before.

That I might require twelve capsules of peyote squash to respond to the genius arrayed before us in the night ahead—Coltrane, Bruce—plainly bespeaks an impulsiveness of appetite, lack of judgment, and so forth. I can't remember anyone referring to excess, although surely the concept existed even in those times.

That afternoon we parked in North Beach, still known as the hipster quarter then. (In contrast, Haight-Ashbury in 1962 was a working-class inland neighborhood, full of inexpensive, pretty Victorian houses, a secret for the locals and the native born.) We made Coltrane's first set before dark. As the half dozen of us staggered in, we could feel the Aztec potion stirring inside us ever so subtly, closing down our frontal lobes, awakening the reptilian brain cells we all shared with the Great Lizard of the Dawn of Time. The Lizard was manifest in the hypnagogic patterns inlaid against our inner eyelids, unmistakably pre-Columbian, an angry Chacmool, scorning the white-eyes' summons.

As we took our table, a wind rose from over the edge of something, tasting of the void. The wind grew in intensity until it fixed us to our chairs and threatened to send our drinks flying. We held on. I affected sangfroid but I knew the wind would never stop, that it had come for me. Its force was unimaginable.

I turned to the stage, where Coltrane was doing "My Favorite Things." I suppose my jaw dropped, that I stood agape. I glorified the Lizard. The Lizard caused the music from the stage to become visible. This is not a metaphor; on peyote there are no metaphors. From the tenor sax issued festive, gorgeous silk bands of the brightest richest red, whirling and dancing and filling the space with scarlet bows and curls. The brass produced great fat waves of frost, ice-lightning it appeared, with a razor-sharp serrated edge—the waves expanding and contracting marvelously along the bass line. From each instrument in its kind issued some manner of bright spectacle, not one of which I could handle remotely. Bracing in the terrible wind, stepping carefully over the bright music that was piling up on the floor, I made for the street. I tried to be cool, and showed everyone who glanced at my walkout a grinning rictus of terror. My extremely loyal Janice came with me, as did a guy, one of our number, who had eyes for her. The three of us trudged around the corner into Chinatown.

This was, you might say, a Chinatown of the mind. It was actual Chinatown, Grant Avenue, but it was more profoundly Chinatown in no ethnic sense. Rather, the Polanski sense of a lost and terrifying cityscape; its clinky, clunky exoticism, designed to divert the tourists, provided me with an experience much richer and stranger—so rich and strange in fact that as I am a Christian faithful man I would not spend another such a night though 'twere to win a world of happy days (*Richard III,* act 1, scene 4). It was like drowning in a vat of the strangest malmsey.

I became persuaded that there was a sharp pain in my foot. I, Janice, and the guy who had eyes for her all went into St. Mary's Square to sit on a bench, at the foot of the statue of Sun Yat-sen. When I took my shoe off it seemed that my sock was drenched in blood— bright blood, the color of John Coltrane's soprano sax riffs. I took my sock off. My foot looked similarly bloodied. It appeared there was a nail in my brand-new Macy's Palo Alto shoe, purchased a day or two before. The nail was pointed *up,* the business end half an inch into my sole, hence the sharp pain.

Across the path from us, a couple of tough-looking Chinese teenagers were providing wolf tickets, close-ended blank menace. As they watched, we began to puzzle out the mystery of the foot, the shoe, and the nail. Something like this scene ensued.

ME: Blood! Shit!

J (six peyote capsules): That's impossible. I mean . . . It's not possible.

THE GUY WHO HAD EYES FOR HER (about the same): Unhh. Blood? Huh?

ME: Hammered! Some . . . hammered. In my shoe.

J: No you're . . . hallucinating. Just look . . .

TGWHEFH: He's hallucinating! You're hammered, ha ha.

(Janice has put her hand to my foot and then into my shoe. Her hand has come out drenched in blood.)

J: That's impossible. Jesus.

TGWHEFH: Is it blood?

ME: Yes! Blood!

(All three stare harder. Then harder still.)

J: Oh my God. Oh my God! (She gets more blood on her hand. TGWHEFH touches her hand, gets blood all over his hand. We stare at our hands.)

J (to me): Jeez, your eyes. Pupils. They're huge!

(All look at each other's pupils in turn and at each other's hands and at their own. They begin to giggle.)

At this the teenagers exchanged thoughtful looks and departed the park. One droll thing about taking peyote in 1962 was that hardly anyone knew such a thing existed. The observers of our obscenely witless behavior had to ascribe it to either alcohol or mental disorder of an extreme sort. I never got to Lenny Bruce's stand-up. And I had wasted my first Coltrane concert with foolishness.

Events of this sort were repeated; there was lunacy, stark terror, much enjoyment. The upside for me was that in the years of my fellowship at Stanford we all—friends, lovers, fellow grad students—saw a great deal of ourselves and each other, which for the most part pleased us mightily. None but ourselves, a small circle of friends, as Phil Ochs put it, would go near us. We grew close.

Later that year, a number of us received LSD sacramentally. The celebrant was Richard Alpert, Ph.D., since known as Baba Ram Dass. Ram Dass in the early days would jokingly refer to himself as "Dr. LSD Jr." Dr. LSD Sr. would be the late Timothy Leary, Ph.D., his partner in acid research at Harvard. One afternoon Ram Dass turned a number of us on to LSD with a lozenge spray, from an atomizer such as that which hoarse or dying opera singers are represented as self-medicating their tonsils.

Among the communicants was Dr. Vic Lovell, the man to whom Ken Kesey dedicated *One Flew Over the Cuckoo's Nest.* Ram Dass had been Vic's mentor in graduate school, and Vic is the man usually credited with turning Kesey on, when the novelist worked as an orderly at the Palo Alto Veterans Hospital, where its results were being observed. The identity of the observers has since been much discussed.

The afternoon, like so many others, was dappled and lovely. A few minutes after we had fixed, I thought I noticed something peculiar about the back of my hand. Peculiar and nasty. A rash of some kind. Spreading. I gave it the lemur-eyed double scope. It refused to go away; rather, it spread its scabrous net the wider. I made the mistake of consulting Dr. Acid Jr. for a reality check.

DR. ACID (ruminatively): When we were in Zihuatenejo one of us developed a rash on the back of his hand. It looked a little like that.

ME: Yes?

DR. ACID: Yes. It spread.

ME: Spread?

DR. ACID: Yes, it spread over his entire body. He thought he was going to die.

ME: So . . . *what happened?*

DR. ACID: As a matter of fact . . . he died.

I pondered each word. The man had died. Suddenly this seemed a little amusing. The Doctor's cultivated serenity, his cosmic disinterest were comical. I began to laugh, uncontrollably. No one else did.

Later, things improved. There was a brushfire, and red or yellow fire engines (who could tell? what was the difference?) and crackling, whining radio equipment. We had not started the fire, but we tried to make the best of it. A beautiful girl sat on a limb playing Bach on her flute until the aromatic smoke of burning leaves drove her down. Horses appeared and chased us until one of the women, an equestrienne, chased *them*.

One party I attended, the establishing event of what it pleased us to call the Suburban Folklife Center, featured a human cat's cradle. "All the thumbs raise their hands," called Gurney Norman, the Kentucky folklorist who was our founder. It was a kind of square dance.

By this time, our community around the edges of the Stanford campus and the writing center had divided over the question of marijuana. Many of us had seen dope up close in urban high schools during the nineteen fifties. In New York it was associated with gangs of the *West Side Story* era; it went with poolrooms next to the el, zip guns, and fighting with torn-off car antennas. In the Navy, I never went near it; the feeling was that apprehension would entail live burial in the dread fortress at Portsmouth, New Hampshire.

During the sixties grass became one of California's bright wonders and increasingly a social shibboleth. In general, people who smoked tended to socialize with others who smoked. It went with music and it went with sex, which counted for quite a lot. When someone unknown was arriving at a party, or had been invited along on some expedition, the question would be "Is he cool?" Which meant did he do dope. This was partly a question of security, since then, as again now, penalties for marijuana could be severe or viciously absurd. But it was also postadolescent snobbery and self-satisfaction. At least it was with me.

Psychedelia became more and more central to our concerns as time passed. Janice continued to help support us by working as a data processor. On one occasion she exchanged some processing, for a foundation that concerned itself with psychedelic drug research, for a free acid trip.

The term "data processing" was unfamiliar then. Eventually, it began to occur to some people that the availability of mind-altering drugs and the rise of the transistor-microchip postindustrial revolution might not be completely unconnected. There was an idiom, an attitude, around both of these developments that was somehow related. A certain bohemian style informed both. Business histories of the time recount that the sixties were a very bad time for International Business Machines, as it then was, holding to white-shirted, Babbitty styles and routines. In Silicon Valley, *Homo ludens* prevailed among the start-ups, the culture of hot tubs and experimental sabbaticals, grad student life continued by other means.

Strange things, a spirit at once elitist and egalitarian, were taking hold. In one of our writing workshops at Stanford, Professor Joshua Lederberg, the Nobel Prize physicist, had come at Wallace Stegner's invitation to address us. I think it was Wally's way of addressing the C. P. Snow dilemma, which was still on the mind of the academy. At Cambridge, Snow had deplored the disconnect between the sciences and the liberal arts. Or maybe the initiative was Dr. Lederberg's. The doctor told us something he thought we should know as writers: that the line between what was human and what was *not* would presently become uncertain. He was thinking of artificial intelligence.

Lederberg's lesson confirmed our sense of plunging into change, a new oncoming world. I, as a high school dropout whose greatest technical achievement was taking Morse code on a typewriter (long division was beyond me), could only fantasize about connections between this apparently unrelated, but somehow mysteriously covert, research. The Stanford Research Institute, which did a great deal of contract work for the government, was interested in arcane circuits of all kinds.

Politics were also newly rich and strange. In New York, the hard Left was still pretty much in ruins, while the Right was essentially out of town. Had the fifties been a time of rigidity and hysteria? Maybe. It depended on where you lived and who your friends were.

Student demonstrations, youthful crowds battling with the police, were things that happened in Trieste as far as most Americans were concerned. In San Francisco they were getting ready to happen *here,* in the immediate post-Eisenhower USA.

San Francisco had always been a big labor town; maybe that was part of it. Harry Bridges and his longshoremen's union had survived both congressional investigations and purges by the AFL-CIO. Ironically, the port was thriving on American involvement in Asian wars, and the union with it. The locals were often ready to lend their sponsorship to Left-minded rallies. There were those who said that many of the victims of the anti-Communist "witch hunts" back east had made their way to the less accusatory atmosphere of northern California, raised their children there. The red diaper babies, second- or third-generation Communists, Trotskyists, and the offspring of various Marxist heretics, were ready to take revenge on Amerika. The wave of payback was strong on the West Coast.

At the beginning, Berkeley, not Stanford, was the center of neoleftist politics. By the time of the Berkeley Free Speech demonstrations, a few years after we arrived, I had regularly been running into officers of the Young People's Socialist League, the SDS, the *Militant,* the Spartacists, the Maoists, the Communist Workers Party, and the Revolutionary Communist Party (not to be confused with the CPUSA). As the Vietnam War intensified, the radical cadres expanded as if in reaction.

It never occurred to me at first that the Stanford Research Institute, with its enormous Department of Defense contracts, might have served as a leading common denominator for factoring the cultural oddities I was enjoying. The breakthroughs in circuitry and transistorizing, so much of the research that led to the formation of start-ups in Silicon Valley, were done at SRI on Defense budget funds. The high-tech plants were spreading down the valley to the south end of the bay, displacing the fruit orchards and their spring blossom storms, the peaches of Santa Clara, the pears of Mountain View. Eisenhower's interstates, built in part to serve the interests of Big Oil, were funded as Defense spending. This smoke-free industrial revolution was displacing Steinbeck's California, even Kerouac's.

It turned out that the lovely liberating drugs came out of the Stanford Research Institute too, funded by the CIA. So the connections I had been feeling, which I had ascribed to mere propinquity, were substantial after all.

In 1943, in Zurich, a Swiss chemist named Hofmann was experimenting with ergot, a parasitic fungus that affects wheat. His purposes were those of scientific husbandry. After work, Professor Doktor Hofmann, pedaling his bicycle over the cobblestones of the ancient city, began to feel peculiar. The ergot had permeated his bare fingertips, and he was suffering from an attack of ergotism, a not unheard-of condition among populations subsisting on transported, sometimes contaminated flour. The effects were known in the Middle Ages as St. Anthony's fire, or the Dancing Mania. The results of ergotism on cognition had been described as "temporary schizophrenia." Some discovered that this replicated madness was not always so temporary, at least not for everyone.

Dr. Hofmann was employed by the Sandoz Corporation. After his report was published, Sandoz was approached by the American Office of Strategic Services, the proto-CIA of the World War II era. U.S. intelligence was interested in obtaining an incapacitating non-lethal compound or perhaps an interrogation tool, a truth serum. Rumors about this kind of stuff filtered into the scenarios of nineteen forties movies and radio thrillers.

One of the places Sandoz and the CIA bestowed their grant

money was the Stanford Research Institute in Palo Alto. The SRI was already working on Defense contracts of all descriptions, and that may have entered into the decision to take the project there. Perhaps the friendly presence of the Hoover Institute played a role. In the early sixties one might see Alexander Kerensky on his way to his office in the Hoover Tower, most spookily resembling his portrayal in *Ten Days That Shook the World*. If he was in the mood for a movie, Dr. Kerensky could have watched his own rise and fall several times a semester on the Poli Sci Department walls.

During my twenties, I understood that I had shared a universal modern experience: the world I had anticipated as a child, daydreamed about and planned adventures in, simply disappeared before I could get to it. At Stanford, between one thing and another, the first novel I had been working on changed its nature under my hands. Conceived as a realistic political narrative, *A Hall of Mirrors* wandered out of the strictly "realist" mode. I decided, I believe, that between "realism" and formalistic experiment there was no substantial difference. Originality was always welcome; experiments worked or they didn't. Language was language and life was life, one tracking, undermining, enlightening the other. Did I need to spend all those nice Sundays experiencing Owsley-quality death and transfiguration to learn that? Maybe.

I had started out under the influence of the first generation of literary moderns. Hemingway bestrode the world then, inescapable. Instead of learning algebra and long division, I had spent my high school years reading and goofing, in the manner of bookish underachievers then as now. I read the books then read, Hardy, Conrad, Waugh, Dos Passos, Wolfe, Fitzgerald. Young people read many or most of the same books now. Earlier it had been Jack London, Ernest Thompson Seton, William Saroyan, the hagiographies of Louis de

Wohl. Does anyone remember, speaking of odd Catholic novels, *Mr. Blue?* Early Faulkner, Robert Penn Warren. A predictable list for anyone my age.

A year or so older than I, Ken Kesey had finished two novels before the sixties were well under way. Altered states certainly influenced his literary imagination in those books, though not to the degree the feds registered in his FBI file. "Subject has finished two books [there followed ludicrous mangling of his first two titles] one about marijuana and one about LSD." That was how it looked from the seat of government.

One thing being around and being the right age in the sixties gave us was the primary sensation of time's wheel. You could catch glimpses of the fourth dimension, now and then see the world turning. People who lived after the First World War had something like that experience; at least that's the story we can piece together from the narratives they've left us. I don't think every modern era is the same in that regard. Maybe we were a case of the delayed-action "postwar." The fifties were full of nervous assurances that things would go back to being the way they had been, although after the confusions of the forties, no one was sure what that had been. Among many there was a sense that the way they had been was not acceptable. Yet times were dangerous, the elders said; they said not to rock the boat.

I can remember where I was when I heard that Kennedy was shot: in a house on a country road by a creek in Santa Clara County, changing the diaper of our second child, my son, Ian. Deidre, our daughter, born in New Orleans, had been a freebie courtesy of Huey Long and his Charity Hospital. Ian was a virtual freebie as well, but at the far more state-of-the-art Stanford University Hospital. So we'd had both of our kiddies on the cheap—at opposite ends of the economic scale.

Later on the day of Kennedy's death my friend Vic Lovell and I drove around the Stanford area, through the suburban paradises and the clusters of bungalows, and the ghetto of East Palo Alto, the town that later decided not to call itself Nairobi. We were checking out popular reaction. It was California, of course, and popular reaction was difficult to locate on the sparsely peopled streets.

At Kepler's famous bookstore we found out that the shooter was a member of the Fair Play for Cuba Committee. A clerk laughed at our dismay. On the street in Menlo Park, people were crying. When we drove over to the student center, the radical element displayed knowing smiles to the unhappy undergraduates. What the radical fringe thought it knew that Thanksgiving weekend I can't imagine.

People of a certain age maintained over many years an illusion that the world somehow darkened after November 22, 1963. As though things had been getting better and suddenly they began to spin out of control. It was sheer illusion of course, even if one believes in some spirit or pattern of history. Which opens the question of what there is of history beyond what people believe after the fact and think they saw.

These were the kind of questions the LSD experience led us to raise. You could dismiss the whole experience as funny light patterns and snapping synapses. But there were times when the drugs seemed to take you down as far and as deep as you extended, to the very bottom of things themselves. How deep that really was, who knows?

So we inherited, in California in the early sixties, some of the headiest plantings in the American grain. The changes (the word "changes" was often heard in those days) in politics and popular culture may have seemed more profound than they were. They were attended by moralizing and vulgarity of all sorts, and they were very unsettling to many. We won a little and lost a lot, depending.

By 1970, there may have been more in the way of threat than promise around. There was a sense in which everybody lost, or at least paid his or her way. The middle Americans, shocked at seeing hysterical rage visited by half-educated youth on their flag, the radical folkies in flat woolly caps appalled to hear Bob Dylan zap out those electric chords at Newport—all were seeing the future of their dreams go down.

The struggle between the CIA and the bohemians over Dr. Hofmann's Promethean fire contains as many ironies as the era affords, I think. Vic Lovell, the intern at Palo Alto Veterans Hospital and Ken Kesey's initiator in psychedelics, was an activist in the Stanford area for many years. The FBI paid the ultimate compliment by calling him to demand information on the abducted Patty Hearst. "You've gotta be kidding," Vic said. But they weren't.

The CIA and its researchers called their experiments with LSD MK-Ultra. That part of the CIA's history is quite fascinating and frightening and appears in a number of well-researched books: *Acid Dreams,* by Martin A. Lee and Bruce Shlain, is one of the most thorough. It should be remembered that many of the people who did research on lysergic acid as a therapeutic tool were working quite legitimately and in good faith. (Interestingly, just as the drug made its way out of Defense research circles to therapy studies in North America, it did the same in Communist-controlled central Europe. The work of Dr. Stanislas Grof in what was then Czechoslovakia is part of the literature.) Their results were not negligible. Many people saw therapeutic uses for LSD-25, and some still do. Experimental grants stand approved by the governments of several countries today, including the United States, for work with Ecstasy and related compounds.

Where these elixirs of the psyche will lead us in the era of chimeras and clones is daunting to speculate. More than forty years have passed since Joshua Lederberg told the writing students that humanity was relative.

After the experiments, when Ken Kesey had written *One Flew Over the Cuckoo's Nest,* he dedicated the novel to the man who turned him on.

"For Vik Lovell," the dedication reads, "who told me that dragons did not exist

Then led me to their lairs."

EIGHT

Ken Kesey worked in a cabin so deep in the redwoods above San Francisco that the indifferently painted interior walls seemed to grow seaweed instead of mold. Even with glass doors, it held the winter light for little more than a midday hour, so the place had the cast of an old-fashioned ale bottle. It smelled of ale too, or at least beer, and dope. These were the days of seeded marijuana; castaway seeds sprouted in the spongy rot of whatever had been the carpet, and plants thrived in the lamplight and bottle green air. Witchy fingers of morning glory vine wound in every shelf and corner of that cabin like illuminations in some hoary manuscript.

Across the highway, on the far bank of La Honda Creek, were more morning glory vines. They were there because Kesey had taken his shotgun and filled the magazines with all the mystically named varieties of that flower's seeds and fired them into the neighboring hillside. The morning glory, as few then understood, is a near relative of the magical *ololiuhqui* vine, used by Chibcha shamans in necromancy and augury and finding small items that have been misplaced. The commercial distributors of the seeds, on record as all unaware, gave the varieties names like Heavenly Blue and Pearly Gates. Once ingested, the poisonous-tasting seeds would produce hours of startling visions and insights. (A warning: Don't try this at home! Morning glory seeds as presently sold are advertised as being toxic to the point of deadliness.)

La Honda was a strange place, a wide spot on the road that descended the western slope of the Santa Cruz Mountains toward the artichoke fields along the coast. Mainly in the redwood forest, it had the quality of a raw northwestern logging town transported to suburban San Francisco. In spirit it was a world away from the woodsy gentility of the peninsula towns nearby. Its winters were like Seattle's and its summers pretty much the same.

Kesey and his wife, Faye, had moved there in 1963, after their house on Perry Lane, in Menlo Park, was torn down by developers. Perry Lane was one of the small leafy streets that meandered around the Stanford campus then, lined with inexpensive bungalows and inhabited by junior faculty and graduate students. (The Keseys had lived there while Ken did his graduate work at the university and afterward.) The area had a bohemian tradition going back to the time of the economist and sociologist Thorstein Veblen, who lived there at the beginning of the twentieth century.

Kesey, as master of the revels sixty years later, did a great deal to advance that tradition. There were stoned poetry readings, also lion hunts on the midnight dark golf course where chanting lion hunters danced to bogus veldt rhythms pounded out on their kitchenware. Drugs played a part, including the then legal LSD and other substances in experimental use at the VA hospital in Menlo Park, where Ken had worked. The night before the houses on the lane were to be demolished, the residents threw a demented block party at which they trashed one another's houses with sledgehammers and axes in weird psychedelic light. Terrified townies watched from the shadows.

I first met Kesey at one of his world-historical tableaux, a reenactment of the battle of Lake Peipus with broom lances and saucepan helmets. (The Keseys' kitchenware often took a beating in those days, though I can't say I remember eating much on Perry Lane.) I attended in the person of a Teutonic knight. Ken, formerly a student at the writing workshop, represented Alexander Nevsky.

When the Keseys moved to La Honda, it became necessary to drive about fifteen miles up the hill to see them. Somehow the sunstarved, fern- and moss-covered quality of their new place affected the mood of the partying. There was the main house, where Ken and Faye lived with their three children, Shannon, Zane, and Jed, and several outbuildings, including the studio cabin where Kesey worked. There were also several acres of dark redwood, which Kesey and his friends transformed little by little, placing sculptures and stringing batteries of colored lights. Speakers broadcast Rahsaan Roland Kirk, Ravi Shankar, and the late Beethoven quartets. The house in the redwoods increasingly became a kind of auxiliary residence and clubhouse cookout—a semipermanent encampment of people passing through, sleeping off the previous night's party, hoping for more of whatever there had been or might be. It was a halfway house on the edge of possibility, or so it appeared at the time. Between novels, Ken had forged a cadre in search of itself, the core of which—in addition to Ken Babbs, who had just returned from Vietnam, where he had flown a helicopter as one of the few thousand uniformed Americans there—consisted at first of people who had lived on or near Perry Lane. Many of them had some connection with Stanford. Others were friends from Ken's youth in Oregon. Old beatniks, such as Neal Cassady, the model for Jack Kerouac's Dean Moriarty in *On the Road,* came around. Some of the locals, less used to deconstructed living than the academic sophisticates in the valley below, saw and heard things that troubled them. This would cause many problems later on.

As Wordsworth wrote, it was good to be alive and to be young was even better. More than the inhabitants of any other decade before us, we believed ourselves in a time of our own making. The dim winter day in 1963 when I first drove up to the La Honda house, truant from my attempts at writing a novel, I knew that the future lay before us and I was certain that we owned it. When Kesey came out, we sat on the little bridge over the creek in the last of the light and smoked what was left of the day's clean weed. Ken said something runic about books never being finished and tales remaining forever untold, a Keseyesque ramble for fiddle and banjo, and I realized that he was trying to tell me that he had now finished *Sometimes a Great Notion.* Christ, I thought, there is no competing with this guy.

In 1962, he had published *One Flew Over the Cuckoo's Nest,* a libertarian fable to suit the changing times. It had been a best-seller on publication, and has never been out of print. The book had also been adapted for a Broadway stage production starring Kirk Douglas, who then proposed to do it as a movie. Ken and Faye had gone to the opening night, in that era of formal first nights, in black tie and gown. Now, a few months later, he had another thicket of epic novel clutched in his mitt, and for all I knew there'd be another one after that.

He really seemed capable of making anything happen. It was beyond writing—although to me writing was just about all there was. We sat and smoked, and Possibility came down on us.

Kesey was, more than anyone I knew, in the grip of all that the sixties seemed to promise. Born in 1935 in a town called La Junta, Colorado, on the road west from the dust bowl, he had grown up in Oregon, where his father became a successful dairyman. At school, Kesey was a wrestling champion, and champion was still the word for him; it was impossible for his friends to imagine him *losing,* at wrestling or anything else. Leaving the dairy business to his brother Chuck, Kesey had become an academic champion as well, a Woodrow Wilson graduate fellow at Stanford.

Ken's endorsement, at the age of twenty-six, by Malcolm Cowley, who oversaw his publication at Viking Press, seemed to connect him to a line of "heavyweight" novelists, the hitters, as Norman Mailer put it, of "long balls," the wearers of mantles that by then seemed ready to be passed along to the next heroic generation. If American literature ever had a favorite son, distilled from the native grain, it was Kesey. In a way, he personally embodied the winning side in every historical struggle that had served to create the colossus that was nineteen sixties America: An Anglo-Saxon Protestant Western American White Male, an Olympic-caliber athlete with an advanced academic degree, he had inherited the progressive empowerment of centuries. There was not an effective migration or social improvement of which he was not, in some near or remote sense, the beneficiary. That he had been born poor, to a family of sodbusters, served only to complete the legend. It gave him the extra advantage of not being bound to privilege.

Some years before *Cuckoo's Nest,* Ken had written an upublished Nathanael West–like Hollywood story based on Kesey's unsuccessful attempt to break into the picture business as an actor. All his life, Ken had a certain fascination with Hollywood, as any American fabulist might. He saw it in semimythological terms—as almost an autonomous natural phenomenon rather than as a billion-dollar industry. (This touch of naive fascination embittered his later conflicts over the adaptation of his novels into films.) However, it was as a rising novelist and not an actor or screenwriter that he faced the spring of 1963. There was no question of his limitless energy. But in the long run, some people thought, the practice of novel writing would prove to be too sedentary an occupation for so quick an athlete—lonely, and incorporating long silent periods between strokes. Most writers who were not Hemingway spent more time staying awake in quiet rooms than shooting lions in Arusha.

Kesey was listening for some inner voice to tell him more precisely what role history and fortune were offering him. Like his old teacher Wallace Stegner, like his friend Larry McMurtry, he had the western artist's respect for legend. He felt his own power and he knew that others did, too. Certainly his work cast its spell. But, beyond the world of words, he possessed the thing itself, in its ancient mysterious sense. "His charisma was transactional," Vic Lovell, the psychologist to whom Kesey dedicated *Cuckoo's Nest,* said to me when we spoke after Ken's death. He meant that Kesey's extraordinary energy did not exist in isolation—it acted on and changed those who experienced it. His ability to offer other people a variety of satisfactions ranging from fun to transcendence was not especially verbal, which is why it remained independent of Kesey's fiction, and it was ineffable, impossible to describe exactly or to encapsulate in a quotation. Fitzgerald endowed Jay Gatsby with a similar charisma—enigmatic and elusive, exciting the dreams, envy, and frustration of those who were drawn to him. Charisma is a gift of the gods, the Greeks believed, but, like all divine gifts, it has its cost. (Kesey once composed an insightful bit of doggerel about his own promises to the seekers around him. "Of offering more than what I can deliver," it went, "I have a bad habit, it is true. But I have to offer more than what I can deliver to be able to deliver what I do."

Kesey felt that his world was his own creature and, at the same time, paradoxically, inevitably, that he was an outsider in it, in danger of being cheated of his own achievement. His forebears had feared and hated the railroads and the eastern banks. In their place Kesey saw New York, the academic establishment, Hollywood. When he was growing up in Oregon, I imagine, all power must have seemed to come from somewhere else. Big paper companies and unions, the FBI and the local sheriff's department—he distrusted them all.

While in New York to see the Broadway adaptation of *Cuckoo's Nest,* Kesey had caught a glimpse of the preparations for the 1964 world's fair. It didn't take him long to dream up the idea of riding a bus to the fair, arriving sometime before the scheduled publication date for *Sometimes a Great Notion.* Somehow, he and his friends the sports car driver George Walker and the photographer Mike Hagen managed to buy a 1939 International Harvester school bus and refashion it into a kind of disarmed personnel carrier, with welded compartments inside and an observation platform that looked like a U-boat's conning tower on top. It was wired to play and record tapes, capable of belching forth a cacophony of psychic disconnects and registering the reactions at the same time. There were movie cameras everywhere. Everyone had a hand in the painting of the bus, principally the San Francisco artist Roy Sebern. A sign above the windshield, where the destination would normally be announced, proclaimed, FURTHUR.

By then there were a number of footloose wanderers loitering around Kesey's spread in La Honda, ready to ride as soon as the paint was dry—just waiting, really, for Kesey to tell them what to do next. It was said later that one was either on the bus or off the bus— no vain remark, mind you, but an insight of staggering profundity. It meant, perhaps, that some who were physically on the bus were not actually on the bus in spirit. It meant that millions were off the bus, but the bus was coming for them. If you were willing to entertain Kerouac's notion that George Shearing was God, that bus was coming for you.

NINE

Early on a fall morning in 1963 I went to the Stanford clinic with what I thought was an errant eyelash. A thin crooked line was segmenting my field of vision, making it impossible to read or write anything. Before the day was out, an unwholesome interior light was burning semaphores into the underside of my eyelids. After hours of huddling in darkened cubicles, following the light point, the bouncing ball, and the little green arrow with a swollen gaze, I was unwell. My eyes felt like a pair of grotesquely enlarged pinballs, poached and spinning, expanding and contracting like evil planets. I knew I would never get any skin back down over the front side of them or get my pupils to stop flashing colors yet unborn.

It was dismaying, and might well have been; according to the creepy invisible doctor who intoned my fate with what sounded like a smiley lisp, I was one unfortunate bozo. He asked me if I thought I had a tumor. No, I said, do you? I was not being impolite, I was asking his opinion. He failed to understand and became annoyed. Did I use drugs? What drugs? I asked, hoping to learn something I really didn't want to know. What drugs did I think? he demanded, the voice from some phosphorescent swamp down south where dogs and dog boys scampered. The mortuary poetics in which he delivered his take on my misfortune might have been consoling to a more philosophical or mature patient. It made the dull catalog of my suspected diseases sound not just terminal but weird, like the skeletal specimens of a mad collector.

What drugs did I take? When I put the subject off he began to recite the possible effects of recreational drugs on the eyes like a hit man's evil auntie calling down vendetta. The man was Poe-esque. He foresaw the need for an operation. He foresaw the likelihood of blindness and death. If I postponed an operation to prevent blindness, he said, I would still have to face it eventually. If I lived for six months I would only want to live another six months. The point seemed to be that it was time to surrender my will.

"You have a beard," he asked me, exploring the murk with one of his lights. "Why?"

"It's an affectation."

He switched on his desk lamp and shook his head in sympathy or incomprehension or something. This was my first clear look at him. He looked to me like a perjuring prosecution witness at a country murder trial. I felt like the defendant.

"You're aware it's an affectation but you wear it anyway. Does that make sense?"

This rhetorical question was presented with a thoughtful clinical inflection, as though to open the doors of my self-perception to insight. I told him I was writing a book, certainly a non sequitur and a dumb answer. I had made some kind of vow not to shave until the thing was finished.

A strangely angelic nurse with golden ringlets at her brow appeared out of nothingness. Or else I had simply not noticed her in the darkness. The doctor addressed himself to her.

"He's writing a book. So he wears the beard." The doctor, visible now as fanged and cross-eyed, allowed himself a chuckle. Suddenly he showed me a toothy leer like the Phil Silvers character in the *Sergeant Bilko* television show of the now long ago. My antagonism and suspicion grew by the moment. Paranoia helped me cope with the humiliation of it all. It helped persuade me that he was lying to me about my condition out of treachery and malice. He was my enemy and I hated him.

The nurse, or whatever she was, had appeared without entering, within a space that had not existed before she occupied it. It suggested the way Kafka's characters in *The Trial* materialize instantly at the margin of chambers that all at once contain them.

"He'll have to shave it off for the mask," she said with satisfaction. Then she turned to me and lowered her voice in a confiding manner. "You'll look better."

Her looks were as disconcerting as her sudden appearance. Her eyes had the jaundiced and metallic shade of the background framing Byzantine saints in Russian icons. The pupils never shifted to settle on a single object; they seemed not to focus. She looked blinded.

I stood up to leave.

"I'll be back in six months," I told them. "To see if I want to go on living."

"It'll be too late," the southern surgeon said.

"Maybe I'll finish my book."

The ethereal nurse began to say something but was silenced, I think, by a cool-it glance from the master. I left the form they offered me unsigned on his desk.

That night I briefly tried not to tell my wife about the interview with Stanford's phantom wizards. Janice and I had few secrets and these usually did not hold up very long. On this particular evening I was weak; I wanted some help in rejecting the eye people's absurd prognosis, someone to complain to and offer something along the order of consolation. So before long I had frightened and distressed this tough-minded and courageous young woman to a point of some extremity. I had also assured myself of shame and remorse over not sparing the girl considerable anxiety that night for the rest of my life—which at least would turn out to be longer than six months. The only upside to this absurdity was a certainty I came to feel that I would never be readier to endure the business of dying than I was at that time. I thought I was handling it pretty well, except for telling her so precipitately about the doctor's routines.

Janice had plans to go back to New York early in 1964; she had enrolled in the spring semester's classes at CCNY. And she was to carry my manuscript—all I had done on it—to Candida Donadio, reputed to be the hottest agent in New York at the time. We decided that the best way of engaging fate was to continue with our plans and see how things turned out.

That fall, the strange, evil weekend of John Kennedy's murder took place. It charged our earthly paradise with a sense of fate and death and reversal of fortune. It was the stuff of children's grief and liberal despair. The radicals at the union read their journals with wise, grimly knowing smiles. Conspiracy theories and sick jokes prevailed. Meanwhile in the quotidian realms of no significance my jagged line turned out to be a hemorrhage inside my eye. Feeling borne on the combined power of ill winds, I ended up in Palo Alto Stanford Hospital, though I never saw the doctor of darkness or his blind angel again.

The less sinister experts with whom I now spoke offered scantily improved hope. Hemorrhages, it was thought, do not appear for no reason. There indeed was the possibility as suggested that I had a tumor, that soon I would be blind, and/or begging for six more months of life. However, the new team seemed to take less pleasure in the fateful and to suggest a more agreeable situation all around.

However, there were diagnostic problems. At this stage of medical history the CAT scan for intercranial examinations had not come into general use. The procedure to be followed was going to consist of two bore holes being drilled into my skull, a business often endured by injured downhill skiers and practiced by the surgeons who serviced them. As I understood it, the method derived from the "trepanning" methods of the pre-Columbian physicians of Mesoamerica and Peru. First the holes must be bored under local anesthetic. Following the procedures current at that time, air would be pumped into the cranial cavity to expedite an X-ray. If a growth or injury requiring surgery was identified, the surgery would come next, part of the same day's work. The more intrusive part of the operation would require deep and total sedation, which was the reason that the exploratory part had to be done on a local. The procedure promised a long day, some risks, and possible surprises. I signed the necessary papers and Janice arranged to fly back west and stay with friends. Of Finnish descent, she might stay close and cast some wholesome sub-Arctic spells. It would be an expensive hassle and an academic inconvenience, because City College in those days was hard work—free of tuition, competitive, and notoriously demanding.

As distraction from her anxieties she smoked a large and varied amount of marijuana before boarding the TWA flight which flew to San Francisco from the newly renamed John F. Kennedy Airport. I remember thinking about the new name at the time: that there was the least too much careless gallantry in it; that it lacked a measure of decent revulsion for ill luck and murder. It was my wife's first flight, and I suggested she try to enjoy it by getting loaded. Friends in California were bringing me some dope to the hospital, a risky business then as now, a time when you could get arrested on your funeral pyre for possession of weed.

During what might have been my last night on earth I was confined in Stanford Hospital in company with a Mormon salesman with a hernia. He was watching television. I had papers to sign, many, and this time I cravenly signed them. I think one of them was a loyalty oath.

"My goodness," my roomie, the salesman, kept saying, "that Mitch Miller is a funny-looking fellow."

Meanwhile Janice, on runway 6 at the newly and ominously renamed airport, had forgotten her mission of mercy. Upgraded by an airline official to first-class, she thought she was on her way home from the opera and kept mistaking the runway lights for downtown Manhattan. We telepathized. I kept imagining her in her boots and deerskin britches, what the world then called "a hippie chick" about to become a cute curvy widow in tight pants high over the Big Sky country. Her new life was in the making, the future balanced literally on a knife edge. I felt horny, jealous, and resentful, about to be cuckolded by death like the late president for whom Idlewild had been rechristened.

The procedures I describe are as I remember them and as they were later explained to me, so I will try to render them as accurately as possible. In the operating theater, I was strung out half upside down on a monstrosity that resembled the Zeiss Stereoptical Projector at the Hayden Planetarium on Central Park West. There were only three of these devices in the world and I was on one of them, a great honor.

"I have to cut into you, Mr. Stone," said the young doctor. "You'll hear it. It'll sound like a dentist drill. But it shouldn't hurt."

My head was shaved, along with my beard. The doc gave me a couple of needles. He and his assistants took up their instruments— surgical knives, drills, hooks, and so on. What they were doing to me did not seem to hurt. As promised, the noise and the vibration suggested dentistry on a monster scale with your head as the tooth. In the mind's eye you were watching someone work a pneumatic drill, waiting for your head to land in your lap.

"I like to sing when I work," the head surgeon said. "You don't mind if I sing, do you, Mr. Stone?"

The main female nurse was a kindly bespectacled English girl, a thinking man's crumpet. I wanted to impress her favorably.

"Under the circumstances, Doc," I said, "I'll take my pleasures where I find them."

My bon mot was a bit of a success. I was pleased but a bit sick at my stomach.

Later on in the procedure, the director of the operation spoke to one of his assistants. "When you cut," he addressed the man sternly, "cut away from the brain."

The procedure would leave me with two holes in my head, since healed but still palpable over forty years later. The reason for two holes rather than one was presumably based on the physical principle that required us back then to make two perforations in a beer can rather than one. This is a principle I vaguely grasp and probably another indication of intelligent design at work on the big picture. Air, inserted and released through these taps, seemed to produce the notes of a steam calliope to replace the rattle of the drill. Maybe I imagined it.

The matter of the mask and my beard never came up because there was no need to remove large pieces of cranium. The condition that had afflicted me was something known to medicine as benign acute intercranial hypertension. Pressure of obscure origin increases in the cranial cavity, causes an effect like a head injury or malignancy inside the cranial cavity, and can cause broken capillaries in places like the eye. The condition is or was sometimes referred to as a pseudo-tumor. No association between drugs and BAIH is known, which of course proves nothing. Anyway, the transformation of the patient's skull into a ceramic flute resolves the pressure. A cure.

Janice stayed in California with me for a while and then went back to New York and CCNY. I walked the streets of Palo Alto skinheaded, proceeding in little tiny steps which rattled every bone between my toes and my molars. I was trying to finish the notorious first novel at an artists' colony in Saratoga, California. By now, I was much encouraged by the fact that the famous Candida Donadio had contacted me. She would take me on as her client. Our relationship was to continue for more than thirty-five years.

Neal Cassady, whom I then knew very slightly, was with his wife, Carolyn, in nearby Los Gatos in a house he had once shared with

Kerouac. From time to time we would share the drive across the Santa Cruz Mountains to Kesey's.

The Santa Cruz were beginning to develop a sinister reputation at that time. In *East of Eden* Steinbeck had found them kindly mountains, compared to the range across the Salinas Valley, which he saw as menacing. The Santa Cruz were certainly beautiful, and magical too. You could pass through vales of fog as thick as woodsmoke and then suddenly come upon a sun-dappled mountain meadow to make your heart soar. In spring the wildflowers abounded as they would in the high peaks of the Cascades. The road between Saratoga and La Honda wound like a fairy-tale lane through redwoods, fields of tule grass, and live oak. Here and there it would pass through valleys filled with ferns that would haunt your dreams.

Unfortunately, we were only a few years short of the Summer of Love, which would fuck everything. Our garden was too beautiful to ever have been free of serpents. Now things were emerging from beneath the earth that created a phylogeny like that at the bottom of Monterey Bay; big ones or poisonous ones were eating little ones. Unlike that on the seafloor, this was a pathological predation, innocence and delusion attracting and setting free murder. Police parlance adopted a sporting metaphor to describe the method of psychos in search of prey. They called it "trolling." The kids talked about "bad vibes." The Santa Cruz became a sinister lonely place.

On reflection, I'm sure this amounts to exaggeration. However, people, especially the young, spoke and imagined in such terms. The fear and attraction became hippie lore, the stuff of urban legend, and so produced some quite real effects. Administrators and residents at my colony at the foot of the mountains became extremely concerned that the gates be locked at night. Returning late and leaving them unsecured was a major dereliction. This was described to me then as a recent development. Fewer and fewer people walked the extensive wooded trails in its arboretum. A young woman was murdered there, on the grounds.

Still, I was not yet ready to abandon my sense of having discovered a new Eden in a condition toward which the entire world ought to aspire. I left for New York again that spring of 1964 because that was where my Heart's Ease dwelled; regrets and dear friendships would not keep me away. Moreover, I thought we would soon be back in California. I resist the idea of ever having been so naive, but perhaps I thought we would return to find everything as we'd left it, waiting to be reclaimed. Maybe I believed that if you worked at it right you could have all the lives you wanted at once, all the loves, all the lights and music.

One true thing about my life in those years was that I was extremely fortunate in the friends and mentors with whose help we made our way. Mack Rosenthal had made me aware of the Stegner Fellowship and accompanied my manuscript with his recommendation. And Wally Stegner arranged for me to meet Dorothy de Santillana, the renowned editor at Houghton Mifflin, when she visited California. She in turn arranged to get me the Houghton Mifflin fellowship for a first novel and a publication contract. When my pseudo-tumor pseudo-struck, occasioning medical bills that would have amounted to a year's income for Darius the Great, Stegner arranged to extend my fellowship so that I was covered by Stanford's health plan. (Wally's recollection of the circumstances under which he worked this out differed from mine. I had hoped to impress this old-time westerner with my cool courage. What he mostly recalled, good-naturedly but not quite so favorably impressed as I had hoped, was my *not* having the tumor I had been so enthusiastically prom-

ised by the goddamn team of blind eye doctors at Stanford Medical.)
My only other option would have been the Veterans Hospital at Palo
Alto, where I might have fallen into the hands of fiendish interns
and orderlies like Vic Lovell and Ken Kesey. I can only hope Wally
(which, by the way, I never called him) didn't really remember me as
a sharper who conned an extra year out of his good-heartedness. The
records are presumably still at Stanford Hospital and should speak
for themselves for anyone interested.

When the term was done, and with it my stay at the art foundation,
I started back east. I didn't have to hitchhike this time or ride any
rails, but the price of an airline ticket was beyond me. I took a Greyhound bus east the day after Barry Goldwater lost the Oregon primary
to George Romney. I'd been riding the Dawg since my mother's first
month as a single mom and it was home on wheels for me.

Once my hair had grown back, along with my affected chin whiskers, I hadn't thought much about my appearance. I was wearing a
secondhand Forest Service khaki shirt, hiking boots, and some spare
socks and things to change into at stopovers. We had rolled no farther than Sacramento when I first sensed the poor impression I was
making on the continent's interior. A stroll around the block near
the Greyhound station seemed to draw the attention of passersby.
Skid row types cursed at me instead of panhandling. Cops grinned
unpleasantly as though entertaining law enforcement fantasies.
When I climbed back in the bus none of the passengers liked me
very much anymore. Was it me? Was it Sacramento?

In downtown Salt Lake City, a team of cops, two of them, gave me
a ticket for smoking a cigarette in Temple Square. One of the officers
suggested I might be wanting a shave. Otherwise I might have more
trouble. On the other hand, he said, I might be looking for trouble.
I might like trouble.

I recalled that the Great Dowser Joseph Smith, whose American Gothic spook house we were at that moment honoring, had liked trouble so much, along with killing people who crossed him and claiming that all sorts of jailbait schoolgirls were his wives, that once upon a time cops like themselves had stood by to allow frontier justice to take its course. He was usually represented as needing a shave too, on the very day of his lynching. I made no historical references at the time. I should mention also that my brief, costly foray around the square afforded me the discovery that Mormons were the most physically beautiful people in the country, maybe the most beautiful of all Caucasians, if Nordics are what you like. Clean living? Good sex? No caffeine? Their affinity for dancing or a gene pool of strivers? I had no time to linger for research that day. The next eastbound Hound left within an hour of my citation, and I chose to be on it.

In Chicago I got off again to walk the streets with my Stanford friend Irving Kupferman. Irving and I had engaged in a rivalry over a woman back in Palo Alto. Then we had somehow taken acid together and become good friends. We were both displaced New Yorkers, and what we liked to do was walk. We walked all over Chicago, so stoned at times we thought we were in some part of New York we'd never seen before. We ended up at an enormous exhibit of contemporary American work at the Art Institute.

I had lived in Chicago with my mother for a while, in a Salvation Army Booth Shelter on the North Side. If I've placed it right, it had been gentrified by 1964 into urban aristocracy. When Mom and I lived there, the kids from the shelter were the only racial mix of kids for miles. Moreover, we were some kind of low-rent Protestant bastards. The neighborhood kids, Poles, Germans—Cubs fans, anyway—made life difficult. One of Lake Michigan's beaches was not far away, but to reach it we had to elude ambush. Of all the kids in the Booth Shelter, the biggest and toughest was an African American girl of twelve or so named Gilda. The Wendish barbarians who pursued us had a reluctance to tangle with Gilda, so as often as possible we Boothies made her our guest at the beach—teaching her to swim, buying her "red hots," as the locals called hot dogs, and ice cream, purchased by pooling our resources. I think some of the kids intimidated other children into contributions.

Anyway, she loved fighting white boys. God, she was bad! She had to be. She was no help against black kids, though; the presence of black male adolescents made her go all funny and shy. However, the neighborhood was so venomously racist that there weren't many black kids. Maybe I'm idealizing Gilda, but I don't remember her picking on anyone who didn't pick on her. She had a great laugh.

It was pretty progressive of the Salvation Army to plunk down a Booth Shelter in that part of town. Nevertheless, I was not fond of the Army. They punished me for teaching other children Go Fish. Cards were wicked and they confiscated mine. They thought my mother had airs above herself and looked down on Salvation Army workers. They were goddamn right about that. Her punishment was nightly pot walloping.

My mother was straight, sexwise, but her inmate pal was a small wizened lesbian with a face like a movie jockey's who knew the ways of the world well enough to make intelligent conversation. Or at least to listen patiently to my mother's version. She was nice to me, this lady. I had never seen anyone like her.

One day, the papers advertised that the sponsors of the Chicago railroad fair were granting free admission to children with over a hundred freckles. Nothing on my face had ever got me anything so far. So I mapped out a route to the fairgrounds and for hours rode the incredible green high-speed trolleys. The guards at the fair gave me a hard time until I thought I wouldn't get in, but they were only kidding. The theme of this 1948 railroad fair as I remember was how wonderful passenger trains were going to be in the future. I can still remember how those brand-new shining coach cars and compartments smelled. It made a kid feel lucky to be born to such an inheritance. I could hardly wait.

The future these railroads were promising us was part of the POSTWAR WORLD, or, as it was frequently known, THE WORLD OF TOMORROW. After a day there I took the wonderful trolleys back to the Booth, and being there didn't bother me a bit. That night Mom and the little jockey lady interrupted their covert two-handed bridge game in the scullery to teach me how the game went.

Irving and I spent a lot of time retracing some of my Chicago hangouts and then he took the el down to the University of Chicago, where he was working. Shortly after, he went to Chile to study in a psycho-physiological program, and I lost touch with him.

By the time I got on the New York bus I was pretty near exhaustion in addition to being ripped on the dope we'd been smoking all day. I bought a pint of ordinary rye at a liquor store next to the terminal, figuring it might provide the balance of energy and relaxation I might require. I had a seat on the aisle halfway back on the bus. I slept for a while. When I woke up I saw a pretty blond girl across the aisle from me. I was not in the mood for hitting on strange young ladies, nor was it something I often did. But she looked across the aisle, saw that I was awake, and asked how long I'd been traveling. I told her pretty much nonstop since San Francisco. She said I looked it, asked me if whiskey helped. I offered her some and to my surprise she took it and helped herself to a fair slug. I saw that she was not as young as I had first thought. Not middle-aged, but not a postadolescent either. She was South African, riding on one of Greyhound's See America cards. She said she loved traveling at night except where you missed the beautiful scenery.

While our conversation flickered along, I was becoming more and more aware of the men sitting in the seats behind us. Boarding, I had seen that they were U.S. Navy sailors. This inclined me favorably toward them in general. I noticed that their neckerchiefs were badly, inexpertly rolled, which let me know that they were unfamiliar with the dress uniform. The sailors wearing their hats had not learned how to bend the outside rims to look squared away. Then I saw that they all had the same rating mark: two white lines parallel at an angle. As I suspected they were boots, that is, recruits just out of boot camp, and since they had boarded at Chicago, it had probably been the Recruit Training Station at Great Lakes, Illinois.

It occurred to me that they had given me sort of contemptuous looks as I got on the bus, the kind I had seen in Sacramento and Salt Lake. But because they were Navy apprentices, and I was an ex–petty officer with a little brace of service ribbons, so dominant in time and rank—I felt—I couldn't take their bug looks seriously. I couldn't help feeling a certain sympathy also. Navy boot camp had softened up by the sixties, but it couldn't have been an easy experience for a young person even then.

I didn't like the way they sounded, though. Not that I was hearing menace, just a kind of nastiness in the rise and fall of their voices. They seemed to have a leader who spoke the way they did, only more unpleasantly. Nor did I care for the kind of stage-whisper vocalizings. Every time I took a swallow of the whiskey, or offered one across the aisle, they would all fall silent.

By the time their whispered exchanges got my attention the South African across the way had gone to sleep. These guys weren't talking to me, but I couldn't help believing they were talking about me. Why? It really didn't make any sense. Did my pint bottle of booze arouse their envy and rage? Did they think I was chatting up a girlfriend? Impossible. So I kept trying to make the talk I was hearing come out differently.

Naturally I have trouble re-creating dialogue I was trying to mis-understand. As I heard it, what they were saying, the young leader and his pals, went something like this:

"Fuggin beatnik, we can teach him to ride right. Who the fug he think he is." This sounded like Pittsburgh to me, the gerund Norman Mailer employed to ease the realistic soldier speech in *The Naked and the Dead* being a common usage in the Steel City. Pittsburgh was always a righteously tough town but never had more than its share of sociopaths. Moreover, the bus wasn't headed for Pittsburgh.

"We can't jump him in the bus."

"Fug, we can't. Nobody sticks up for fuggers like that. See people lookin' at him funny? With the booze and tryin' to make the [woman]."

"We could kill the fugger."

A thoughtful silence ensued. No one laughed although I waited.

"We could," the same voice insisted. "There's just yams back here."

Most of the passengers in the middle of the bus were black. Yam, I knew, was American street Sicilian for blacks. Whether it was more universally used in Pittsburgh I couldn't say.

"They wouldn't do shit. The yams? They wouldn't see nothing, ya know it? Noaw. They just set back and be cool and don't see nothin' and don't remember nothin'."

This came with a mixture of racist dialect comedy and complacent admiration. Another youth then said:

"I don't want to kill nobody."

"Then whadya jern the Navy fer?" the leader asked, sounding upset.

I was trying about as hard as I ever had to reject the evidence of my senses. How could anyone have the bad luck to end up on a bus full of homicidal morons and become the object of their violence? Finally I stopped trying to not hear these ravings and went to work on a strategy. One rule of counterambush: Take the initiative. Always know a little more about what will happen next than your opponent, if possible. Start it yourself. I had figured out who the leader was. The way was to walk back there and double-talk down into his face until he ran out of energy and looked like a jerk to his friends. Sucker-punch him if necessary. I knew all this from some experience. But it was I who was running out of energy, with my road visits and boozings. I did a sensible adult sort of thing, and of course it doomed me.

I walked up to the driver and told him that sailors in the seat behind, about six of them, I figured, were planning to assault me.

"Why?" As he took his eyes off the road long enough to ask me this, I could see enough of his face in the night lights to realize that he sort of understood why. I was tempted to ask him his theory. But all at once I got it—Sacramento, Salt Lake, here and there in Chicago, beatnik, wrongo. The wars were heating up, the one in Vietnam, the one against white supremacy, the culture wars, as we have learned to call them. I was behind enemy lines, overtaken by the opening attacks, outnumbered.

The driver told me that he was connected by radio band with the police. It sounded as much like a threat as reassurance. Then, having misplayed my weak card, I went back to my seat. All was silence. The recruits appeared asleep. A while thereafter they started whispering together and the guy I thought of as the leader, the youth who did the talking, walked up to the driver. He looked back in my direction, appearing innocent, confused, and hurt. He and the driver had a quick exchange and ended up laughing together. This was not good. As the boot passed me on the way to his seat he leaned down close to my ear and whispered very softly: "Fuggin faggot!"

The rule I had learned was don't let anything like that pass. Respond or it will be the worse for you.

"You talking to me?" I asked as grimly as I could in those days before Bob De Niro.

"Fag," he whispered again. I liked the way he kept his voice low. On the considerable downside, it looked to me like what was coming next was a charge that I had propositioned him or his pals. There was a small coterie of servicemen who picked up money robbing homosexuals who approached them for sex. The defense always put forth was the defense of manly virtue. This lowlife and his band did not seem to have been in the Navy long enough to have taken this up. To paraphrase Hemingway, they did not know they were queer-rollers yet but they would find out when the time came. If they made a move, that would be their story. I would then learn how to ride right, if they had the good sportsmanship not to kill me.

Eventually, we pulled into the next rest stop. It was in a town just over the Pennsylvania line from Ohio, a town whose name I will not forget and a place I think about, though briefly, pretty much every day. Highspire, PA. Makes a pretty sound when the locals say it with their whiny diphthongs.

It was still dark when we filed into the fluorescent glare of the service counter. There was a separate area with tables and a little sign over the entrance that said Servicemen and Teamsters Only. It reminded me of signs I'd seen in some towns that lived off the Navy that read Whites Only followed by No Dogs or Sailors. In jolly Highspire attitudes were simple.

I got the sense that people in the place, bus passengers and other customers, truck drivers, waitresses in their blue-and-white gingham uniforms, and of course my onetime shipmates—the lot of them—were eyeing me. Some people had stayed inside the bus to sleep.

Inclined as I was to empty my bladder, I didn't want any part of that place's men's room. That was where I'd get it. Some of the privileged teamsters were already in humorous conversation with the sailors. Cooks and pearl divers would open the service door to the counter from time to time, anticipating some amusement.

I wasn't going into the gents but I figured I could find a discreet place outside. I paid for my undrunk coffee and went out. Naturally I saw myself as the center of all attention. What, who, was there to talk about in Highspire, PA, in the darkness before dawn?

I pissed in the shadows of the lawn in the rear of the building. No damage done, but it had been a stupid move, illegal and throwing me open to all kinds of dirty-minded prosecutions, for which, in those enlightened days, people had their houses painted red or burned down.

The sky was beginning to lighten. The highway carried scant morning traffic between two wooded ridges whose eastern peaks were just visible in outline. To the west the crests disappeared into darkness and fog. It was cold and I was tired, too cold and tired to realize how angry I was. I was probably less angry than I might have been because the improbability and absurdity of the circumstances made them difficult to focus on.

The cold reminded me that I had left a jacket on my seat in the bus, and my impulse was to keep my possessions in one place. I went back aboard and grabbed my jacket and also my old Navy seabag in which I'd stowed everything I owned, including the manuscript of my ongoing and ongoing first novel. The Navy recruits were scouting the grounds for me. When they saw me climbing out of the bus with my stuff they started yelling. One of them said I had his seabag, and maybe he thought I had. People sleeping in the bus woke up and looked out. Customers and help crowded to the diner windows.

The sailors had taken off their jumper, the uniform top that is worn instead of a shirt, and were stripped above the waist to T-shirts. An elderly lady who'd come out of the diner clucked concern over the lads' exposure to wind and weather. She had a buddy, another elderly lady, to console her.

"Oh," the other old bitch sighed reverently, "they're used to it." Then both old bitches resumed bug-looking me and squawking to the driver that I was holding some brave young sailor's seabag. While the crowd surrounded me I had to show the driver my Naval Reserve ID. To match the serial number on the bag. By law I had been transferred into the Naval Reserve at discharge, so I owed the Navy some inactive time. Wondrous to behold I was a brave young sailor too, beard and outrageous costume notwithstanding. So I crashed through the encircling citizens while the boots shouted after me and ladies screamed. A bunch of truck drivers were standing beside the diner door watching the passengers reboard. A couple of them came up to me. One of the guys looked over his shoulder as though checking for witnesses. There were plenty of witnesses, white, black, young and old.

"Where you going?" said one of the truckers.

"Are you talking to me?"

"That's right."

The Greyhound was getting into gear. I was holding my possessions in both hands. I set them down.

There followed a pointless hostile exchange in the course of which we all moved from the path of an oncoming vehicle. This left us closer to the truck parking area. The first punch of the night got thrown, a sucker punch right out of the movies which was directed at me but missed. At this point I realized that the passing vehicle was what had been my bus. I saw the happy sailors and their mentor who gave me a series of triumphant grimaces, the touring South African, puzzled, and the concerned elderly ladies, wreathed now in fatso smiles. All gone, but leaving me without a bus and with a contingent of speed-addled drivers with a beef.

"I seen you in Chester!" one of the drivers shouted. "You was with them niggers in Chester."

All I knew about Chester, excepting that I had never been there, was that it was somewhere outside Philadelphia in a different part of the state from Highspire. I later learned that there had been a demonstration there, an antiracist demonstration for jobs or housing. As had happened down south, I was being mistaken for a more generous spirit, someone more actively concerned with justice than I seemed to be. At least I didn't deny it.

Denying it would not have bought much. Closer to the big trucks, on the teamsters' turf, I was not doing well. My one scoring point, perfectly legitimate in parking lots, was an elbow to the mouth of a guy who was trying to steal my bag from between my feet. But that was it, from then on it was them over me and I was covering up, on one side with my knees up, my vital organs as secure as I could make them, clinging to the seabag that contained the manuscript of the great work in progress. I was still getting kicked when it got light and the sun mounted the peaks of Highspire, PA.

I thought it might be dark again before I put the goddamn place behind me. Forget hitchhiking; I had a ticket! Half a dozen times I had to read the small print on the ticket aloud into the life-embittered, overtrafficked face of some Greyhound jock before my blood-spattered, half-mad ravings persuaded one man he had better let me on his bus if living was what he had planned on. So we had to ask a very old non-English-speaking lady to change her seat, and the driver had to move his squared-away braided cap and his briefcase from the seat beside him, replacing them with me.

I don't remember much after that. Janice had got us an apartment on West Ninety-seventh in Manhattan. It had two windows on an alley and the services of a screeching maniac who sounded off about every four hours 24/7 and could freeze the blood of a naive subject in his or her veins. By a naive subject I mean a person who had never previously heard the madman report.

Friends of ours tell us that the place was the ugliest apartment we or anyone they knew for that matter had ever lived in. This may be true. But I was very glad to see it and to see she who would for many years bear the burden of my sneering jokes at the sights it occluded and the sounds it would so regularly admit. Bear them as she had borne the two kiddies who were now jammed with us in the tiny pad. And on we went. My head healed from being drilled and kicked on. Janice got her degree cum laude and worked for the welfare department. And one day on the kitchen table, while Cousin Brucie was spinning the Zombies' "She's Not There" and the loony was sounding his four o'clock alarm, I finished the final pages of *A Hall of Mirrors*.

Seaman's papers,
New Orleans, 1960.

Near the Luxembourg Gardens,
Paris, 1964.

The USS *Arneb*, en route to the Antarctic, 1957.

Janice in 1964.

Expatriated in London, 1969.

Janice with our daughter, Deidre,
in Menlo Park, California, in 1962.

Me, Janice, and Deidre at San Gregorio
Beach, California, in the summer of 1969.

Ian and Deidre on the grass, and a
curious bird.

Playing with Ian.

Ken Kesey at his writing desk in
California.

Proto-Pranksters feasting on Perry
Lane, circa 1962.

Kesey at his studies, during the bus trip to
New York.

Cassady, driving *Furthur*.

The bus *Furthur*, with Kesey stationed on top, and Neal Cassady at the wheel.

Pranksters at the Nut Shoppe in Manhattan: Dale Kesey, Ken Babbs, Ken Kesey, John Babbs *(lighting cigars in back)*, Chuck Kesey, Neal Cassady, and Paula Sundsten.

Jerry Garcia and Pigpen playing at
San Francisco State University in 1966.

Neal Cassady posing with service posters in Manhattan.

Allen Ginsberg in
the early sixties.

George Walker in full psychedelic regalia.

Ken Kesey *(left),* and Jack Kerouac *(below)*: two American authors in a reflective mode.

At a New Orleans cemetery during the 1969 filming of the movie *WUSA*, based on *A Hall of Mirrors*.

In the Jones Library at Stanford, 1963.

TEN

Like everything that was essential to the sixties, the Kesey cross-country trip has been mythologized. If you can remember it, the old saw goes, you weren't there. But the ride in Ken's multicolored International Harvester school bus was a journey of such holiness that being there—mere vulgar location—was instantly beside the point. From the moment the first demented teenager waved a naked farewell as Neal Cassady threw the clutch, everything entered the numinous.

Who actually rode the bus, who rode it all the way to the world's fair and all the way back, has become a matter of conjecture. The number has expanded like the opening-night audience for *Le Sacré du printemps,* a memorial multiplication in which a theater seating eight hundred has come, over time, to accommodate several thousand eyewitnesses.

Who was actually on the bus? I, who waited, with the wine-stained manuscript of my first novel, for the rendezvous in New York, have a count. Tom Wolfe, who did not see the bus back then at all but is extremely accurate with facts, has a similar one. Cassady drove—the world's greatest driver, who could roll a joint while backing a 1937 Packard onto the lip of the Grand Canyon. Kesey went, of course. And Ken Babbs, fresh from the Nam, full of radio nomenclature and with a command voice that put cops to flight. Jane Burton, a pregnant young philosophy professor who declined no challenges. Also Page Browning, a Hell's Angel candidate. George Walker. Sandy Lehman-Haupt, whose electronic genius was responsible for the sound system. There was Mike Hagen, who shot most of the expedition's film footage. A former infantry officer, Ron Bevirt, whom everybody called Hassler, a clean-cut guy from Missouri, took photographs. There were two relatives of Kesey's—his brother Chuck and his cousin Dale—and Ken Babbs's brother John. Kesey's lawyer's brother-in-law Steve Lambrecht was along as well. And the beautiful Paula Sundsten, aka Gretchen Fetchin, Swamp Queen.

To Ken, to America in 1964, world's fairs were still a hot number. As for polychrome buses, one loses perspective: the Day-Glo vehicle full of hipsters is now such a spectral archetype of the American road. I'm not sure what it looked like then. With Cassady at the throttle, the bus perfected an uncanny reverse homage to *On the Road,* traveling *east* over Eisenhower's interstates. Like *On the Road,* the bus trip exalted velocity. Similarly, it scorned limits: this land was your land, this land was my land—the bus could turn up anywhere. If the roadside grub was not as tasty as it had been in Kerouac's day, at least the grades were better.

Ken had an instinctive distaste for the metropolis and its pretensions. He was not the only out-of-town writer who thought it a shame that so many publishers were based in New York, and he looked forward to a time when the book business would regionally diversify, supposedly bringing our literature closer to its roots in American soil. But the raising of a world's fair in the seething city was to Kesey both a breath of assurance and a challenge. Fairs and carnivals, exhibitional wonders of all sorts, were his very meat. He wondered whether the big town would not trip over its own grandiose chic when faced with such a homespun concept. Millions were supposed to be coming, a horde of visitors foreign and domestic, all expecting the moon.

The bus set off, sometime in June. Nineteen sixty-four was an election year. To baffle the rubes along their route, Ken and Cassady had painted a motto over the psychedelia on the side of the bus—"A Vote for Barry Is a Vote for Fun"—hoping to pass for psychotic Republicans hyping Goldwater. The country cops of the highways and byways, however, took them for Gypsies and waved them through one town after another. Presumably, the vaguely troubled America that was subjected to this drive-by repressed its passing image as meaningless, a hallucination. Sometime around then someone offered a lame joke in the tradition of Major Hoople, something about "merry pranksters." (Major Hoople—a droll comic-strip character at the time, the idler husband of a boardinghouse proprietress—was one of Cassady's patron gods.) The witless remark was carried too far, along with everything else, and for forty years thereafter people checked for the clownish fringe at our cuffs or imagined us with red rubber noses.

Eventually, the bus pulled up in front of the apartment building on West Ninety-seventh Street, in New York, where Janice and I were living with our two children. Suddenly, the place was filled with people painted all colors. The bus waited outside, unguarded, broadcasting Ray Charles, attracting hostile attention with its demented Goldwater slogan. We and our kids took our places on top of the bus, ducking trees on our way through Central Park. Downtown, a well-fed button man came out of Vincent's Clam House to study the bus and the tootling oddballs on its roof. He paused thoughtfully for a moment and finally said, "Get offa there!" That seemed to be the general sentiment. Other citizens offered the finger and limp-wristed "Heil Hitler"'s. Later, the gang drove the bus to 125th Street. The street was going to burn in a few weeks, and, but for the mercy of time, some pranksters would have burned with it.

There was the after-bus party where Kerouac, out of rage at health and youth and mindlessness—but mainly out of jealousy at Kesey for hijacking his beloved sidekick, Cassady—despised us, and wouldn't speak to Cassady, who, with the trip behind him, looked about seventy years old. A man attended who claimed to be Terry Southern but wasn't. I asked Kerouac for a cigarette and was refused. If I hadn't seen him around in the past I would have thought this Kerouac was an imposter too—I couldn't believe how miserable he was, how much he hated all the people who were in awe of him. You should buy your own smokes, said drunk, angry Kerouac. He was still dramatically handsome then; the next time I saw him he would be a red-faced baby, sick and swollen. He was a published, admired writer, I thought. How can he be so unhappy? But we, the people he called "surfers," were happy. We left the party and drove to a bacchanal and snooze in Millbrook, New York, where psychedelics had replaced tournament polo as a ride on the edge.

The bus riders visited the world's fair in a spirit of decent out-of-town respect for the power and glory of plutocracy. They filmed everything in sight and recorded everything in earshot. Like most young Americans in 1964, they were committed to the idea of a world's fair as groovy, which in retrospect can only be called sweet. Sweet but just the least bit defiant. Also not a little ripped, since driver and passengers had consumed mind-altering drugs in a quantity and variety unrivaled until the prison pharmacy at the New Mexico state penitentiary fell to rioting cons.

And, of course, the fair was a mistake for everyone. Now we know that world's fairs are always bad news. In 1939, the staff of a few national pavilions in New York had nothing to tell the world except that their countries no longer existed. The hardware of national geegaws and exhibits went as scrap metal to the war effort. In 1964 the fair produced nothing but sinister urban legends in unsettling numbers, grisly stories of abduction, murder, and cover-ups. Children were said to have disappeared. Body parts were allegedly concealed in the sleek aluminum spheres. It was the hottest summer in many years. Some of the passengers were so long at the fair that they went home without their souls. Jane, the philosophy professor, insists to this day that she made it to the fair only because she had lost her purse on the first day of the trip. Back in California, she became a mother and went to law school. Kesey and Cassady went home too. Fame awaited them, along with the same fascinated loathing that Kerouac and Ginsberg had endured. We couldn't imagine it at the time, but we were on the losing side of the culture war.

The sorry spectacle in Flushing Meadows in the summer of 1964 might be remembered as the last world's fair. There were other, later, hyped-up gatherings of the sort, but 1964 was the one that somehow let the air out, the last attempt to generate enough fatuous futuristic optimism to float such a promotion. The parched sweating queues, the sinister rumors and paranoia, the bad news from Southeast Asia and America's decaying cities, all seemed to underline in irony a message that "the world," as an entity, had little incentive for self-celebration. In retrospect, it seems well that Janice and I chose that summer to get ourselves to Paris. Paris was where we would have gone a few years before, had we possessed the wherewithal. We had chosen New Orleans then, settling for a town that offered the advantage of being a Greyhound bus destination. By the summer of 1964 we had saved and borrowed the price of some transatlantic tickets. In July of '64, along with several thousand other American tourists, we arrived at the Gare du Nord.

Our college friend Michael Horowitz was beginning his career as a dealer in rare books and had a job at Paris's premier English-language bookstore, known in those days as Le Mistral. Its proprietor, George Whitman, was of that generation of Americans who had settled in Paris right after the Second World War, a group that included the founders of the *Paris Review* George Plimpton and Blair Fuller, and writers such as James Jones, William Styron, and James Baldwin. The bookstore commands one of the most outrageously romantic locations in Europe, on the rue de la Boucherie across a little square from the Church of St.-Julien-le-Pauvre. Its windows face the river on the quai de la Tournelle, directly across from the flying buttresses of Notre Dame.

As some of us do, Michael fell heir to a destiny so incredibly unlikely that his future condition seemed to embody just about every element in American life that he then earnestly repudiated. In those days, however, he shuttled around Europe, buying first editions for the shop and sometimes literally minding the store when George was otherwise occupied.

Those of us who have the uneasy pleasure of knowing George Whitman are familiar with his mercurial disposition and his generosity. When we arrived in Paris, through Michael, we were able to take up the offer that George sometimes extended to impecunious writers in the city, the use of a bed on the shop's upper floor after its midnight closing time. The weeks we spent there were not many but they served as our introduction to what remained of the city people like us had so long daydreamed about. They also provided our slim but heartfelt claim on a little of the Paris nostalgia that should sweeten the youthful remembrances of any American writer.

In the summer of 1964, opposing Algerian factions were still actively planting bombs on their fellow countrymen. Charles de Gaulle had instituted the Fifth Republic, ruling in the name of order, and the gendarmes, their capes weighted with coshes like the flippers of homicidal penguins, turned out regularly to brawl with the students who turned out regularly to protest whatever you had got. One day an American poet friend turned up at the store shaken. He had just rescued his small daughter from in front of a police charge outside the Luxembourg Garden, where she had been licking an ice-cream cone, oblivious of the oncoming juggernaut of law enforcement bearing down on her like the Wrath of God Express.

It seems hard to believe that all this was something over forty years ago, as I write. If we could have looked back forty years then we would have seen the summer of 1924, Ernest and Hadley Hemingway visiting Gertrude Stein and Alice Toklas on the rue de Fleurus, James Joyce dining at Lipp's. But the Paris I remember from 1964 seems recognizably balanced between the way points, the decorous yet rakish city of the twenties expatriates and the steam-cleaned, expensive city of Diane Johnson's marital narratives.

About the time of our first stay George Whitman had changed

the name of his establishment from Le Mistral to Shakespeare and Company. Quite appropriately he was assuming the imprint of Sylvia Beach's bookshop on the rue de Seine which had played so important a role in the expatriate scene of the nineteen twenties. As Shakespeare and Company, Whitman's store has carried on Beach's traditions, providing a hangout, sometime hostel, and lending library for Anglophone writers and students of literature in English. For nearly fifty years Whitman's Shakespeare and Company has been a daily destination for lonely English speakers making a home for themselves.

Today the neighborhood behind the bookstore is quite gentrified and spiffy. In 1964 it was a raw, heavily immigrant part of town where Arab music could be heard far into the night in narrow courts. The rue de la Huchette was then as now a nighttime draw for traveling youth and the odd juvenile delinquent, but the fast-food and pizza joints were yet to come. The appearance and feel of the streets back from the river was still a touch medieval, the rooftops inclining to meet over cobblestone streets in a manner to intimidate and beguile the imagination. The blocks of the student quarter and the gray buildings of the Sorbonne stetched inland toward the Pantheon and the place Maubert. All through this part of Paris were dozens of cut-rate hotels, some of them charging as little as two dollars a night, all of them packed during the summer with North Americans equipped with Arthur Frommer's travel books that purported to guide the purchaser through his days in Paris at the rate of five dollars. Some of these places were truly squalid and literally verminous but others were clean and cheerful. The nice ones seemed always to employ middle-aged ladies in blue aprons who could be seen each morning, their hefty frames filling the narrow stairwells, trudging up the stairs one step at a time, maneuvering trays full of fresh croissants and pots of coffee past the tight turns. That part of town had some of Paris's most fashionable restaurants but there were also bistros where the steak frites cost a fraction of what the same menu might demand in New York. Good wine delivered to the door was cheap enough to lure the abstemious and ruin the indulgent. This I suppose would also have been the Paris of Godard's *Breathless,* whose ultra-American ingenue-temptress, played by Jean Seberg, lived at the Hotel Californie and sold *Herald Tribune*s on the street. It was also a quarter that for the denizens of Shakespeare and Company was presided over by the genius of Samuel Beckett, who we knew lived not far away in Montparnasse. One evening Michael and I set out to actually find the great man. What we wanted from his presence was unclear to us even at the time. Maybe we thought he would treat us to a Pernod and a line-by-line explication of *Molloy.* We had heard that Beckett frequented a certain café and it seemed that this might be the place to run him down. I think we further nourished a picture of the divine Beckett surrounded by his characters, drinking plonk with Nag and Nell and Vladimir and Estragon and of how we might pull up a couple of chairs and join them to ponder the meaninglessness of life in opaque evocative aphorisms. We actually located the place on the boulevard Montparnasse and got as far as the door. At that point we registered that the café, with hedges and murals and glistening Bar Americaine, was not the sort of place that would have welcomed Nell or Estragon or us, or even Beckett perhaps, before he had copped his Nobel Prize. We returned to the bookstore that was home.

Talking to teenagers in contemporary France (I could probably say "modern" France to differentiate the present from the land of my antique recollections), I find they have trouble imagining how things were forty years ago. Staying in Shakespeare and Company in the early sixties was immersion in various quotidian aspects of Paris that were distinctly odd to the American sensibility. The building that houses the shop is now a model of renovation, a structure maintaining its medieval Parisian exterior while furnished with every mod con. In the days I'm recalling the plumbing was as timeless as the chimney pots, consisting of a deep sink that served all floors and a convenience with foot-contoured platforms that enable those occupied there to keep their balance over the bottomless hole in the floor. Bathing was surrounded with rituals that made it doubly appreciated, since it consisted of an expedition over the footbridge to the Ile St. Louis and the public baths and the modest expenditure of two francs. One franc's admission, fifty centimes for a towel, and a tip of fifty centimes more for the attendant, and the customer received a franc's worth of hot water for a shower. It may have been worth as much to check out the bathhouse alone, a brick edifice that was a monument to nineteenth-century social justice and resembled the morgue in every silent movie version of *Svengali*.

In the store we browsed and chatted, waiting for closing time so we could go upstairs and claim our assigned sleeping spaces among the second-story shelves. This could on occasion assume some aspects of a lottery if George, carried away by hospitality, had welcomed one or two more indigent scriveners than there were beds. At least once our friend Michael found that the *patron* had taken pity on a homeless street dweller and assigned his space to the *clochard*. Most nights, though, Michael could count on a comfortable kip from the wee hours until opening time the next day. We didn't talk much about dreams so I don't know if Michael had any. If he had I doubt they gave any clue to the future, a future in which he would have a beautiful daughter whom he would name Winona and who would become an internationally famous movie star under the name of Ryder, and that her lovely face and form twelve feet high would be on display at the Cinema Odeon a few blocks from our lodgings at Shakespeare and Company.

On certain nights we would buy some kif from the Algerian hustlers in the back streets and then, in the hours after midnight, tune in Radio Luxembourg. Across the river, visible through the enormous second-story window, was Notre Dame. The cathedral's towers, spires, and buttresses were deliriously floodlit, and we would feast our eyes on the beauty of the place, sipping wine, tripping on fond absurdities, and generally rejoicing in the good fortune that had placed us so wonderfully at the center of our childhood dreams. Life sometimes can be subsumed in magic, although the supply is not inexhaustible. One time it touched us was during that summer in Paris. A little of that shimmer will always flicker in our hearts.

ELEVEN

The offices of the paper I will call the *National Thunder* were located, in 1965, a few blocks down Fifth Avenue from the Flatiron Building. The *National Thunder* was one of several publications that comprised a chain of imitation magazines and newspapers known as Universal News. They were imitations in the sense that their masthead names and cover layouts closely resembled those of other, better-known and more popular publications. Universal News's informing strategy was the hope of confusing a distracted and overstimulated public into buying its periodicals by mistake.

The lord of this empire of the ersatz was a man called Fat Lou. Lou had half a dozen of these replicant outfits, ringer schlock magazines whose names were bogus household words. As an admirer once put it: "If there were a magazine named *Harper's* Lou would start a magazine called *Shmarper's.*"

"Mine are better," Fat Lou would often say.

Maybe his most successful publication was what Fat Lou's lawyers defined as "a weekly tabloid with a heavy emphasis on sex." This was the *National Thunder.* It was an imitation of the *National Enquirer,* lacking the delicacy and taste of the original. Indeed, it offered readers an emphasis on sex, but an even greater emphasis on the bizarre, not to say the freakishly improbable.

All Fat Lou's wonders—the illusion of a modestly vast press cartel—required the combined labor of about ten men and women. We often pondered what ironizing aspect of fate had brought us, in mockery of our fading youth and bright hopes, to the crummiest end of Grub Street. There, in the dank basement of hackdom, lived the *National Thunder,* and there it was I labored.

Actually, it was malicious fun to show a copy of the *National Thunder* to new hires and watch their lips tremble. "Now, the look of the publication may shock you," we'd explain. If it didn't it wasn't for our lack of trying. Eventually we lost all decent restraint.

Three of us put out the *Thunder* and each of us claimed some degree of leftist credentials. One of my colleagues was a Maoist mime, who served as a one-man politburo, providing social consciousness as required. "Armless Veteran Beaten for Not Saluting Flag" was one of his headlines. He also wrote the daily horoscopes under the byline Haji Baba, which allowed him to derive principles such as surplus value from the journeying of the stars. ("Don't be afraid to ask for a raise, Sagittarius! Your boss always keeps some of the value of your labor for *himself!*")

Another was a passionate young man who went about in a similar stage of outraged political excitement and who resembled the late actor Zero Mostel.

My own specialty was the composition of headlines, and my weekly aspiration was to make the front page. The trick of the tabloid front page was to combine a lascivious or revolting photograph with a headline at least equally arresting of attention. Hack writers come and go, but a good art department, one that can reliably fake pictures from the photo library, is irreplaceable. It is not true, however, that one sleazy picture is worth a thousand inflated words.

Hemingway would always say that he learned his trade at the *Kansas City Star.* With this in mind, I should pause for a little reflection on what I learned at the *National Thunder,* beyond the depths of vulgarity of which I was capable. Certain laws obtain in all fictive enterprises, low journalism included. They are almost moral laws, the way grammar in its way is moral.

I have come to believe that language, a line of print, say, is capable of inhabiting the imagination far more intensely than any picture, however doctored. The same principle applies to the novel, if it works. No Hollywood flick, no movie of any provenance, can ever provide an experience of the battle of Borodino as intense as that provided in Tolstoy's pages. Descriptive language supplies deeper penetration, attaches itself to the rods and cones of interior perception, to a greater degree than a recovered or remembered image. Language is the process that lashes experience to the intellect.

I learned this working against deadline, trying to get an old horror-movie still to work as my front page. Our one-person art department, serving the entire Fat Lou realm, was Natasha, an artist of great effrontery and skill. Our prospective cover was the head shot of a slain lady vampire. In order not to limit possibility and make the fantasy our own, we asked her, the art department, to ink out the fangs. In the process she had an accident; ink covered everything. Time was running out; the mats had to go to Jersey to be printed inside of half an hour. Our front page was a distressed-looking starlet whose mouth was a mass of slop. In black and white, the ink looked for all the world like blood.

I started playing with ghastly headlines, sizing them in. All at once, driven by hysteria, by Satan, by my Friday afternoon craving for a paycheck, suddenly I had it:

MAD DENTIST YANKS GIRL'S TONGUE

By God, it fit like a nail! Still, it remained to write the story, and I wanted this one for myself.

Dateline: Podunk, Alaska, or Gondawooleroo, NSW, or Bluebell, Delaware. Anywhere that didn't exist. We maintained an atlas to avoid the accident of hitting on an actual place. By now the readers (*you,* ladies and gentlemen, not the readers of the *National Thunder*) will have surmised the great redeeming element in our work. What kept us on the right side of madness was this: that as lousy as the world might be, though life might condemn us to the sick soft underbelly of journalism, things were not quite so awful that the lunatic nightmares we fashioned had any direct connection with reality or, as it is sometimes called, truth.

Anyway, this just in:

—A beautiful young model, suffering an impacted wisdom tooth in this isolated desert community, was the victim of a ghastly mutilation yesterday. Overcome by periodontal pain while driving by Egg Drop, she called at the office of the town dentist, Dr. Homer Creel. Rendering his patient unconscious, he proceeded to work his ghoulish "surgery." Speaking with great difficulty at Yoof City Animal Hospital, the model, Miss Letitia Fumpton, fought bravely to describe her ordeal.

"He told me something," she said, on regaining consciousness, "something about discomfort."

Creel was taken into custody by the Federal Fish and Wildlife Service.—

(Here space and custom required a picture of Dr. Homer Creel. Working against the clock, we shuffled through our gallery of pictures of creepy people. The weirdest, nuttiest person we could find represented was a nineteenth-century novelist. Since the novelist had never been a resident of Utah, at that time the only American state in which dead people could sue, we were home free. Dr. Creel's head shot did not even require doctoring; his period attire was to be taken as a function of his eccentricity.)

Our foto file had many morbid pictures of deceased individuals undergoing the gruesome horrors of decomposition. There were also many portrait pictures of people in the fullness of health. Some of these portraits, with a little alteration, could be passed off as anyone. Like Dr. Homer Creel, for example, the predatory periodontist. We used Generalissimo Francisco Franco as Haji Baba, the progressive astrologer. Trotsky had a role too, I remember, as a slumlord brained by one of his own defective bathtubs. Woodrow Wilson was the horse handicapper, a role undertaken in real life by one of Fat Lou's cronies.

Identity was a protean and unstable element around the *Thunder*. We could combine an action shot with a grinning cadaver or terrified victim-to-be, a vehicle, a harness, what-have-you, all spliced by the genius of Natasha in the art department, into a form that told a very grim story indeed. Thus:

SKYDIVER DEVOURED BY STARVING BIRDS

And lickety-split there it was and you could hear the clacking beaks and the echoing screams of the doomed sportsman, his features ripped warm and bleeding, his fingers clawed from the harness by the hunger-crazed kites and corbies, not four-and-twenty but thousands! All this above the horrified upturned faces of the watching crowd!

———————

As the weeks went by, bringing the due date of our next possible unemployment checks, we pulled out all the stops. At one point, some zany state's attorney general, with nothing better to do than read scuzz tabloids, inquired into one of our stories, EXPLODING CIGAR KILLS NINE.

The AG was ready to prosecute. We had to explain that just as names were changed to protect the innocent in our newspapers, so also circumstances were adjusted, that the order of facts or even the facts themselves were conceived in such a way that no one should suffer embarrassment. The light went on in his brain after a moment. Our sales were interdicted in his state, which, we had to remind him, contained no such town as Ding-a-Ling.

One day, going up in the elevator, I saw Alger Hiss. And it wasn't like thinking you saw Joe Hill; he was really there. All at once I registered the presence of a tall, professorial man in a faded brown fedora. In each hand, he carried a dark leather bag which might have been a sample case. It was a stormy day. His hat brim was turned down and the morning rain ran onto the narrow shoulders of his raincoat. His stance was braced against the weight of the cases, which imposed on him a Willy Loman–like submissiveness; he was the portrayal of reduction and humiliation. Still, I thought his face was marked with a certain irony, the curled bloodless lips, the arched eyebrow. So sacrificial a figure he appeared, so accepting of his suspension from grace, that he gave off a sort of *darshana,* like the Christus in some Popular Front crucifixion by Philip Evergood. He and I were the only people in the elevator.

I wanted to turn around and say something. Maybe I wanted to spin suddenly and say, "I know you didn't do it, Mr. Hiss." Or maybe I wanted to say: "I always knew you did it, commie!" Maybe I wanted to ask him: "Did you do it, Mr. Hiss? You can tell me." I'd ask for an interview.

All the rest of the day I went around telling people that I'd seen Alger Hiss in the elevator. It proved a conversation stopper.

A few weeks before this tour of the corporate workplace ended, before I qualified for unemployment insurance again and could go back to work on my novel, I got hired away from the *National Thunder* by a rival tabloid. I have trouble believing this represented any kind of professional recognition. However, two of the three of us from the *National Thunder* found ourselves working across town at a somewhat higher salary.

The atmosphere at the *Inside Scoop* was different from that at the *National Thunder*. Though the word fits uneasily, one might have called it more authentic. It was not and did not attempt to appear a "chain." The product was unitary, a tabloid on the pattern of the *National Enquirer*. Like its model, it sold sex and grotesquerie, though its inclination was toward show business and the rising celebrity culture. Its most distressing aspect, from the staff perspective, was that some of the stories behind the headlines were more or less true; that is, events related to the ones in the story had actually occurred somewhere in the real world. These developments were always regrettable, and the notion that they had befallen actual people, or reflected human behavior, was disturbing.

Sometimes informants or aspiring paparazzi showed up at the offices with tips or compromising photographs. The man who ran the paper I call the *Inside Scoop* had once been notorious for his gossip magazine. He had figured in a major Hollywood libel suit, and on one occasion an outraged reader gunned him down—real pistol, real bullets, real time. By the time I went to work for him, however, he was fading into relative obscurity, and his A-list of "showgirls," "profiles," and high-living gangsters was dissolving into morning-after mist. He himself had come to inhabit a ghost town peopled by phantoms of the Great White Way.

To Big Bob, the most important man in town was Walter Winchell, to whose friendship and patronage he generously ascribed his own top position. This was in the period not long before Winchell's death, when the Stork Club, W.W.'s column, big-time radio, and even the *Daily Mirror* were all things of the past. In Big Bob's book, though, Winchell was bigger than Norma Desmond, and nothing lay beyond his powers of good or evil.

Of Bob's media glory, it seemed only this imitation tabloid remained, and I remember a wistful sense of reduced circumstances around the offices. The place had been engineered from a former milliner's loft, a mere pistol shot's distance from Bloomingale's. As for me, a reasonably educated person with pretensions to a high calling, a family man and a father of young children, it was pitiful and, God knew, a moral and intellectual humiliation as well as a treason of clerkery and worse.

It was a shame how some of the stories were true. But the fact was that the old *Scoop,* with its overworked, underpaid staff of heads, hipsters, players, and urban frontiersmen, its doctored, covert, and disgusting photographs—the shameless lies and the shameful authenticity—kept me in a state of unsound euphoria. It was the first job I ever held down where drugs were consumed during working hours—exempting the half pints of Gold Leaf cognac that rewrite on the *Daily News* consumed between midnight and dawn. The skewed mortuary glamour of Big Bob's operation, the Runyonesque shadows and flashes, held me bound in fascination. In retrospect, the associations I made between absurdist extravagance and controlled substances would cause me some trouble down the road.

Having dodged or at least survived a bullet in the service of an unfettered press, Bob often entertained a large, elegantly suited man who looked as though he had illuminated a few disputations in his day. The big fella was known at the *Scoop* as Richie Construction, which was either a derivation of his name or his corporate identity. In any case, Richie knew and admired Walter Winchell, had made himself invaluable to the great man many times, and had a vast store of "Walter stories." All Walter stories had the same general significance at their core, namely the obsessiveness of Winchell's revenge, his vast mechanisms of control and readiness to injure anyone, no matter how pathetically powerless or well intentioned that person might be, in retaliation for the most ephemeral slights.

Richie had explanations for many things that had been a feature of life in his era, from the ineluctability of Walter Winchell's vengeance to the origins of organized crime. The creation myths of the two were identical.

"The smart people worked it out. Somebody makes a mistake— they gotta pay." He would recount this cheerless message with a sad shrug and a sigh. He had, Big Bob assured us, often appeared as the herald of smart people's displeasure.

The *Inside Scoop* gave employment to both the smart and the less so. With everyone imagining himself hip to the scene, in debt to bookmakers, dope dealers, loan sharks, and even honest creditors, with a vague lingering scent of long-ago shakedowns, blackmail, and violence, frictions developed that sometimes threatened to abrade and contuse. There was rather too much fraternization. Wives and girlfriends, husbands and boyfriends, were always getting in trouble and being thrown out. Sometimes they would seek refuge with other couples, which could compound everybody's trouble.

One melancholy example of misunderstanding involved three friends of mine and brought to bear all the increasingly unstable elements of the era: racial tension, the sexual revolution, and feminist autonomy. Reduced to its common denominators, however, it was no more than the eternal down-low shit, timeless at its core.

X., a staff writer with the *Scoop* who rendered elegant, erudite, and delightfully ironical prose with a sophisticated Afro-American flavor, found himself temporarily unhoused. He was given refuge by Y. and Z., a husband and wife respectively, employees of the *Scoop*. All at once Y. found himself working overtime, taking over as chief editor, compelled to spend more and more time late in the office. Big Bob may have planned this as a sort of revenge (for something unknown) in depraved hope of the outcome, namely that unattended, Z. and X. would drift into a romantic liaison. So the outcome came out.

One night Y. arrived home to confront a scene of dishonor, X. and Z. unclad, in bed. Y. was a hot-tempered man, somewhat overweight, but not unfit for strenuous activity and surprisingly fast over short distances. He happened to own a staple gun, not your little notebook stapler but a giant roofer's staple gun, good for shooting giant metal hooks to bind steel. Good, Y. thought, for shooting into X. to impress on him, or in him, Richie Construction's principle: You make a mistake, you gotta pay.

X. comprehends the gestalt. He's up and gone. Wisely, he has not paused to be stapled. Nor has he paused to dress. X. wears nothing but sharkskin loafers as, pursued by Y., with the big staple gun shooting barbed horseshoes at him that blast two-foot plaster craters in the hallway walls, he hurtles down the apartment building's stairs. Once down, there remains only the street. It's cold out. X. is wearing only his sharkskin loafers, nothing more. Y. flings himself down the stairs, still pursuing, still firing giant staples. X. has no choice but to flee through the winter streets, Y. gaining on him as he loses a loafer on the turn.

There are few people out, it's very late, it's the Upper West Side. Dog walkers and such folk. They have nothing to say to the frantic, half-tumescent young black man running toward them. People scream. Behind X. lurches a hyperventilating fat man, waving what looks like a machine gun. It's Y., something out of condition from all those late-night deli sandwiches eaten at his desk at the *Scoop*. The police, the old-type insensitive, unimaginative police, arrive. And there's more, but no matter. It was all unfortunate, and very mischievous of Big Bob.

The *Inside Scoop* provided a personal dimension that was not likely to be available at just any cheesy tabloid. One of the oddest of its homespun touches was the presence of Bob's two sisters. They were actually sisters, Bob's and each other's, two of them, and though I would be hard put to render their job descriptions or even, at this passage, to remember each lady's name, I will never forget their voices. This is because their voices, reading every writer's story aloud, were the usual vehicles of judgment at the *Scoop*. I will call them Grace and Maude, not their real names.

Procedures differed from over at the *Thunder*. We composed some headlines, but we received assignments too. An assignment might come from Bob, from the sisters, or even from Richie Construction. Richie's were tediously moralizing and spun themes around the same plot: People make a mistake for which they gotta pay. Failing to recognize Walter Winchell was a common faux pas in Richie's fables, or failing to recognize some button man and to render deference. Richie did give us a nice story about two drunk *capos di regimes* having a live crab-eating contest at the Fulton Fish Market, scooping the things right out of their barrel. This will suffice, I think, to illustrate why invented stories are so liberating and bright with possibility, while the true shit keeps you bound to a fallen world.

Bob himself liked a story of mine. It was invented, but in its perversity and cruelty might well have been true. It goes like this: Man spends his life buying numbers tickets. Every day for fifty years he plays the bolito, blanks every time. One day—his birthday—he hits the big one. He calls his wife. She's "Oh come home before something happens!" He goes "Ha! I'm gonna celebrate." Maybe he buys a beer at the corner. Maybe he goes to buy a lap dance. He comes out on the street, he's giddy. Here comes the truck. Splat!

What's this in his bloody hand? Unreadable. The winning bug gets swept in the sewer, the birthday boy goes to the morgue.

What Bob and Richie liked was my headline: HE'LL NEVER SPEND A DIME! They went around repeating it for days. "NEVER SPEND A DIME!" Losers couldn't win was the whole of the law to those guys.

The sisters, Maude and Grace, had similar attitudes. Of course, as women, their concerns were more sensitive to relationships, the emotions, the nuances of romance, the play of the errant heart.

One day Maude and Grace gave me an opportunity to prove myself on their court, which was, finally, where the big decisions were made. They assigned me a story from the glory days of the old magazine, evoking the grand old times. They did it, I guess, to see if I was a true player.

Few careers have identifiable low points. Shakespeare himself tells us: "the worst is not so long as we can say: this was the worst." But this was bad. I was assigned a cover byline and a false identity. The best I can say of the project is that it was a kind of social investigative story, to the extent that invented stories of no consequence about unreal and dead people can be called investigative. Anyway, it was an exposé, one where you pronounce the final *e*.

My cover byline was Carmen Gutierrez. I was, Carmen was, "a sexy Latin showgirl." The story was called RUBIROSA WAS A FIZZLE IN MY BED!

Porfirio Rubirosa, as mercifully few will now remember, was a "playboy." (See *Playboy* magazine for variations on the term. The word "playboy" had slightly obscene undertones when it was current, but nothing like the dirty diminutive infantilism it suggests now.) Rubi, as fellow trashy international socialites may be imagined addressing him, was a friend/creature or something of Winchell's. And vice versa. He had supposedly represented the Dominican Republic at the United Nations while that country was under the rule of the surreally sadistic General Rafael Leónidas Trujillo. Rubi was always in the columns, especially Winchell's. Press agents for the splashy nightclubs of the time, the Stork, the Copa, El Morocco, constantly reported his dancing away the nights at their establishments, whirling successions of heiresses and celebrities until dawn.

As presented, Rubi was to be envied in every way, but the subtext was his prowess as an indefatigable lover. People like Richie and Bob and the guys who ate live crabs at the Fulton Fish Market would discuss what they had heard were his techniques. One was to keep one hand up to the wrist in the iced champagne bucket to delay orgasm. All over New York, parochial-school freshmen, Navy recruits, apprentices at the Metallic Lathers Union were filing that one away to use when they took Zsa Zsa to the Pierre and someone showed them an ice bucket.

Thus, the given was Rubi's well nigh mystical prolongations, the whisper current in every high-tone powder room, the very prospect of which cast beautiful women of every conceivable eminence at his feet. I, however, knew better! I, Carmen Gutierrez, author of the *Scoop*'s exposay, was going to set the world straight!

Maude and Grace oversaw as I rolled the sheet into my typewriter. I had not thought that it would come to this. Every life, every career, has its lowest point. I was hoping this would be mine. RUBIROSA, I typed somberly, WAS A FIZZLE IN MY BED! By Carmen Gutierrez.

"Do you really think 'fizzle'?" I asked Maude. She had written the headline for me. "Don't you think something else . . ."

" 'Fizzle'!" she told me. "I want 'fizzle'! 'Fizzle' says it!"

Fizzle, right.

I will pass over, forget, those writerly tropes I employed to breathe life into Carmen. Let's call her a Latin Bombshell. Irrepressible! Volatile. Enthusiastic. And Fun! Oh, and when she got a load of Rubi, ay ay ay! Handsome? Caramba!

That's how Carmen was. An original.

There followed volleys of innuendo and cute euphemism to the effect of my—Carmen's—disillusionment, repeated until my hand began to wither and my tongue cleave to the roof of my mouth. I handed the copy to Maude for the showdown.

Maude walked with a cane. She was stocky and blue haired. She would spend all her time at the end of a blond table next to a pile of legal pads. I watched her eye the story. Everyone in the shop grew silent. Then Maude threw back her head and gave voice.

She read the title in a voice of pleasant expectation. She carried on with the lead, in the same tone. She was beaming. I was very ashamed. So awallow in humiliation and self-pity was I that I failed to notice that at a certain point in the narrative her voice had begun to trail off. Her reading began to sound like a tape recorder with its battery running down. Or, as we used to say, a record at the wrong speed. She kept looking between the sheets in her hand and me, as though I were out of my mind. This annoyed me, since it had hardly been my idea to pose as Carmen Gutierrez, and express wry disappointment at the manhood of an elderly Dominican. Everyone else was equally silent. Maude was shaking her head. Across the office, X., the thief of hearts, restored to his clothes and safe from Y.'s revenge, and Richie Construction were laughing at my annoyance.

After fixing me with a snakefish eye, Maude pretended to make an effort to read more. It seemed heavy going. She put a hand to her throat as though her vocal cords were seizing up. Then she gave up and simply stared at me.

"What's wrong?" I asked her. "I mean, that's what you asked for."

She exchanged a look with her sister Grace and shook her head in silent hopeless denial.

"Kid," she said. "Aw, kid."

Kid was what she called me, although I was practically thirty.

"What, for God's sake?"

"What?" she raised her voice and nearly shouted at me. "Put some *pizzazz* in it! That's what! Put some *pizzazz* in it."

I felt like Raskolnikov contemplating the value of Kempskaya's life, the scant reasons for enduring the old woman's continued existence.

"All right," I said. "I'll run it through again."

I kept my eyes on the paper in the roller. Clickety clack clack I go. After what seemed an hour, I had hacked my way through another take on the idiotic polo-playing skirt-happy impotent son of a bitch and his ditzy unsatisfied muchacha. Once again I handed it to Maude. This time Sister Grace intercepted.

"Let me try it," she said. So she did. In a voice that was softer and more high-pitched than her sister's, she began to read aloud from my tale of Rubi and Carmen, star-crossed sensualists denied their full measure of amor. Grace's reading had a tone of naive sweetness, whereas Maude's rendering had been world-weary and wry. All the same, trying to look as though I were paying no attention, I became aware of Grace's flagging efforts. She had started out all delightfully, full of merry brio and guileless clarity, as warmly confidential as the liver pill salesman on *The Romance of Helen Trent*. All at once her jaw seemed to thicken. The words dragged on without inflection. It seemed one sentence had no connection to another. Carmen's worldly insights were rendered in leaden, labored syllables. Finally, her reading stopped, as though borne down by its weight. She seemed to struggle for breath. It was as though she tried to go on but failed. Then she shook her head, trying to catch my eye and deliver the same bad news her sister had pronounced.

"Kid, Jeezus Christ. That ain't it!"

Big Bob spoke from the raised desk where he presided. "Would yez tell him," he asked Grace, "to put some *pizzazz* in it?"

She seemed stunned by the convergence of insights.

"This is what I'm telling him, Bob!" She fixed on me. "Kid," she said, "you got to put some *pizzazz* in it."

Reimagining Rubi and Carmen, once more visualizing their scented love chamber, I wanted to make them die, just as surely as I wanted to make Grace and Maude and Big Bob and smiling Richie Construction die, howling in the land of Bosch's garden. How could I write of love, or even unconsummated concupiscence, when all I knew were bitterness and rage? I was playing Cupid for these damned perverted defunct conceits, an organ grinder's monkey with a typewriter. I was flashing horrid cupids, grotesque putti with tattoos and crossbows. I was working for Big Bob and the *Inside Scoop* and I'd be doing it for the rest of my worthless dime-a-line life.

But I finished the stupid thing. Every phrase, I knew, was precisely what she wanted. I waited, trembling with anger, for her crone's voice to croon fatuous approval. It had been an act of immolation. I felt as though I had shoved my own pen down my throat. But it was as required.

Grace took the four pages and read through them. This time through, though, she was silent. Her face betrayed no response. After going over the copy deliberately, she passed it to her sister. Maude read it as well and also, curiously, in silence. I watched them whisper together. I was, finally, openly interested.

Maude and Grace turned matching senescent smiles on me. They shook their round balding heads in a unity of rejection.

Grace was the elder, I think; she leaned forward.

"This is just filth," she said.

TWELVE

The culture war got meaner as the world got smaller. Ginsberg and Kerouac, in the fifties, had been set upon by illiterate feature writers concocting insulting lies about their personal hygiene and reporting the clever wisecracks that famous people were supposed to have delivered at their expense. Now the drug thing was being used to make the wrongos feel the fire. At the end of the fifties, Cassady, who was not exactly the Napoleon of crime, had done two years in San Quentin for supposedly selling a few joints. Sometime after Kesey's return to California, in 1965, his house in La Honda was raided during a party. The native country he had just visited in such state was biting back. Ken and some friends were charged with possession of narcotics. Then, on a San Francisco rooftop one foggy night, while watching the Alcatraz searchlight probe the bay's radius, he was arrested again on the same charge. At this, he and his friends composed a giggly, overwrought suicide note addressed to the ocean. ("O Ocean," it began, grimly omitting the *h* to indicate high seriousness and despair.) Fleeing south, Kesey made it to the same area in Mexico where Ram Dass and other such prototypical acid cranks had conducted their early séances.

In New York I got a telegram that declared "Everything is beginning again," an Edenic prospect I had no power to resist. I had finally finished my novel, but it would not be published for a year, and I was at the time employed by what our lawyers called "a weekly tabloid with a heavy emphasis on sex." I had not published anything much beyond "Skydiver Devoured by Starving Birds" and "Wedding Night Trick Breaks Bride's Back," fables of misadventure and desperate desire for the distraction of the supermarket browser. Nevertheless, I was the only person *Esquire* magazine could find who knew where Kesey was. By then, his work and his drug-laced adventures in a transforming San Francisco were well known. *Esquire* paid my way south.

It was the autumn of 1966 and Ken, Faye, their children, and some of their friends were staying near Manzanillo. In 1966, the Pacific coast between Zihuatanejo and Puerto Vallarta did not look the way it looks today. The road ran for many miles along the foot of the Sierra Madre, bordering an enormous jungle crowned by the Colima volcano itself. The peak thrust its fires nearly four thousand meters into the clouds. At the edge of the mountains, the black-and-white sand beach was so empty that you could walk for hours without passing a town, or even the simplest dwelling. The waves were deafening, patrolled by laughing gulls and pelicans.

Today Manzanillo is Mexico's biggest Pacific port and the center of an upscale tourist area. In those days, it seemed like the edge of the world, poor and beautiful beyond belief. One of the hotels in town advertised its elevator on a sandwich board outside. Manzanillo's commanding establishment was a naval base that supported a couple of gunboats.

The Keseys' home was a few miles beyond the bay in a complex of three concrete buildings with crumbling roofs, partly enclosed by a broken concrete wall. We called one of the buildings the Casa Purina. Despite its chaste evocations, the name derived from the place's having once housed some operation of the Purina company, worldwide producers of animal feed and aids to husbandry. In the sheltered rooms, we stashed our gear and slung our hammocks. We occupied our time seeking oracular guidance in the I Ching and pursuing now vanished folk arts like cleaning the seeds from our marijuana. (Older heads will remember how the seeds were removed from bud clusters by shaking them loose onto the inverted top of a shoebox. Since the introduction of seedless dope, this homely craft has gone the way of great-grandma's butter churn.)

Our landlord was a Chinese-Mexican grocer, who referred to us as *"existencialistas,"* which we thought was a good one. He provided electricity, which enabled us to take warm showers and listen to Wolfman Jack and the Texaco opera broadcasts on Saturday. No trace remained, fortunately, of whatever the Purina people had been up to between those whitewashed walls.

We were an unstable gathering, difficult to define. The California drug police, whatever they were called at that time, professed to believe that we were a gang of narcotics smugglers and criminals, our headquarters hard to locate, perhaps protected by the local crime lords. In fact, we were a cross between a Stanford fraternity party and an underfunded libertine writers' conference.

We had no nearby neighbors except the grocery store, and most people along the coast hardly knew we were there, at first. The Casa was far from town, and there was little traffic along the intermittently paved highway that wound over the Sierra toward Guadalajara. It consisted mainly of the local buses, whose passengers might spot our laundry hanging in the salt breeze, or glimpse our puppy pack of golden-haired kiddies racing over black sand toward the breakers. Several times a day, the gleaming first-class coaches of the Flecha Amarilla company would hurtle past, a streak of bright silver and gold, all curves and tinted glass. With their crushed Air Corps caps and stylish sunglasses, the Flecha Amarilla drivers were gods, eyeball to eyeball with fate. Everything and everyone along the modest road gave way to them.

In appreciation of the spectacle they offered, these buses sometimes drew a salute from Cassady. He would stand on a ruined wall and present arms to the bus with a hammer, which for some reason he carried everywhere in a leather holster on his hip. How the middle-class Mexican coach passengers reacted to the random instant of Neal against the landscape I can only imagine. Sometimes he brought his parrot, Rubiaco, in its cage, holding it up so that Rubiaco and the Flecha Amarilla passengers could inspect each other, as though he were offering the parrot for sale. Cassady in Manzanillo was extending his career as a literary character in other people's work—Kerouac had used him, as would Kesey, Tom Wolfe, and I. The persistent calling forth and reinventing of his existence was an exhausting process even for such an extraordinary mortal as

Neal. Maybe it has earned him the immortality he yearned for. It certainly seems to have shortened his life.

People who live in the tropics sometimes claim to have seen a gorgeous green flash spreading out from the horizon just after sunset on certain clear evenings. Maybe they have. Not I. What I will never forget is the greening of the day at first light on the shores north of Manzanillo Bay. I imagine that color so vividly that I know, by ontology, that I must have seen it. In the moments after dawn, before the sun had reached the peaks of the sierra, the slopes and valleys of the rain forest would explode in green light, erupting inside a silence that seemed barely to contain it. When the sun's rays spilled over the ridge, they discovered dozens of silvery waterspouts and dissolved them into smoky rainbows. Then the silence would give way, and the jungle noises rose to blue heaven. Those mornings, day after day, made nonsense of examined life, but they made everyone smile. All of us, stoned or otherwise, caught in the vortex of dawn, would freeze in our tracks and stand to, squinting in the pain of the light, sweating, grinning. We called that light Prime Green; it was primal, primary, primo.

The high-intensity presence of Mexico was inescapable. Even in the barrancas of the wilderness you felt the country's immanence. Poverty, formality, fatalism, and violence seemed to charge even uninhabited landscapes. I was young enough to rejoice in this. On certain mornings when the tide was low and the wind came from the necessary quarter, you could stand on the beach and hear the bugle call from the naval base in the city. Although it had a brief section that suggested Tchaikovsky's "Capriccio italien," the notes of the Mexican call to colors were pure heartbreak. They always suggested to me the triumphalism of the vanquished, the heroic, engaged in disastrous sacrifice. Those were the notes that had called thousands of lancers against the handful of Texans at the Alamo, that had called wave after wave of Juárez's soldiers against the few dozen Foreign Legionnaires at Camarón. Had the same strains echoed off the rock of Chapultepec when the young cadets wrapped themselves in the flag and leaped from the Halls of Montezuma to defy the Marines?

Does any other army figure so large in the romantic institutional memories of its enemies? All those peasant soldiers, underequipped in everything but the courage for Pyrrhic victories and gorgeous suicidal gestures. Naifs led by Quixotes against grim nameless professionals with nothing to lose, loyal to their masters' greed.

So our exile provided more than a hugely spectacular scenic backdrop. The human setting, never altogether out of view, was ongoing conflict. Quite selfishly, we loved the color of history there, the high drama—man at his fiercest. We imagined it all flat out, as presented by Rivera, Orozco, and the rest, the dark and light, La Adelita, El Grito, Malinche. Hard-riding *rebeldes,* leering *calaveras,* honor, betrayal, the songs of revolution. We had ourselves an opera. Or, as someone remarked, a Marvel comic. The concept of real life was elusive. All this naturally gave our own lives a quality of fatefulness and melodrama. We were fugitives, after all—at least Kesey was.

The thing we failed to grasp in 1966 was that Mexico was a nation at a turning point. Time and geography had caused it to require many things of the United States, but a band of pot-smoking, impoverished *existencialistas* who danced naked on the beach and frightened away the respectable tourists was simply not one of them. Gradually, as our presence made itself manifest, it drew crowds of the curious. Young people, especially, were fascinated by the anarchy, the lights and the music. The local authorities became watchful. At that time, marijuana was disapproved of in Mexico, associated with a low element locally and with the kind of unnecessary gringos who lived on mangoes and whose antics encrimsoned the jowls of free-spending trophy fishermen from Orange County. From the start, I think, the authorities in the state of Colima understood that there was more hemp than Heidegger at the root of our cerebration, and that many of us had trouble distinguishing Being from Nothingness by three in the afternoon. At the same time, a sort of fix was in: Ken was paying *mordida* through his lawyers, enough to deter initiatives on the part of law enforcement.

We were bearing witness, unwittingly, to a worldwide development that had begun in the United States. The original laws forbidding classified substances had been framed in the language of therapy, emphasizing the discouragement of such addictive nostrums as "temperance cola" and cocaine tonics. From the fright tabloid to the police blotter the matter went, providing the founding documents of a police underworld, featuring informers, jail time, and the third degree. The resulting damage to American and foreign jurisprudence, the outlaw fortunes made, the destroyed children, and the gangsterism are all well known. What had been a way for Indian workmen to reinforce the pulque they drank and sweated out by sundown, a disagreeable practice of the hoi polloi, became, once it was established as a police matter, Chicago-style prohibition on a global scale. Nothing, travelers found, so preoccupied stone-faced cops from Mauritania to Luzon as the possibility of a joint in a sock, hash in a compact.

In Mexico, we failed to interpret the developments on the drug front to such a degree that when a Mexican plainclothes policeman—Agent Number 1, as he described himself—appeared to make awkward probing conversation with us in the local cantina, we were more amused at his stereotypical overbearing manner than alarmed. We should have seen the deadly future he represented.

Some twenty years earlier, Cassady had brought Kerouac down to Mexico and revealed it to him as the happy end of the rainbow. In *On the Road,* Kerouac records the dreamy observations of Cassady's character, Dean Moriarty, as he provides his *compañero*—Jack, in the role of Sal Paradise—with lyrical insights into a Land That Care Forgot, Mexico as a garden without so much as the shadow of a snake.

Sal, I am digging the interiors of these homes as we pass them—these gone doorways and you look inside and see beds of straw and little brown kids sleeping and stirring to wake, their thoughts congealing from the empty mind of sleep, their selves rising and the mothers cooking up breakfast in iron pots, and dig them shutters they have for windows and the old men, the *old men,* are so cool and grand and not bothered by anything. There's no *suspicion* here, nothing like that. Everybody's cool, everybody looks at you with such straight brown eyes and they don't say anything, just look, and in that look all of the human qualities are soft and subdued and still there.

In 1957, I had sat in the radio shack of the USS *Arneb,* a young sailor with my earphones tuned to Johnson and Winding, reading all this in the copy of *On the Road* that my mother had sent me. If it seems strange that my copy of this hipster testament came from my mother, it would have seemed far more improbable—at least to me—that I would one day be sharing the mercies of Mexico with some of the characters from the book. Nor would I have believed that anyone, anywhere, ever, talked like Dean Moriarty. I was twice wrong, and, as they say, be careful what you wish for.

As we sat in the cantina, watching Agent Number 1 grow more drunk and less convivial with every round, I began to see that Dean

Moriarty and his author had been mistaken in some respects. In the bent brown eyes of the agent I beheld grave suspicion, and my own thoughts began to congeal around the prospect of waking up to breakfast in a Mexican jail.

There were working-class taverns in Mexico (and some pretty fancy ones too) where the drinking atmosphere seemed to change over a few hours in a manner somewhat the reverse of similar establishments in other countries. For example, a customer might arrive in the early evening to find the place loud with laughter and conversations about baseball or local politics and gossip, the jukebox blaring, the bartender all smiles. Then, as time progressed and the patrons advanced more deeply into their liquor, things would seem to quiet down. By a late hour, the joint, just as crowded, would grow so subdued that the rattle of a coin on the wooden bar might attract the attention of the whole room. Men who had been exchanging jokes a short time before would stand unsteadily and look around with an unfocused caution, as though reassessing the place and their drinking buddies. These reassessments sometimes seemed unfavorable, at which point it was time to leave.

Thus it went with Agent Number 1. He showed us his badge, and indeed it was embossed with the number 1, and he assured us that, as cops went, he was numero uno as well. He told stories about Elizabeth Taylor in Puerto Vallarta—how her stolen jewelry was returned at the very whisper of his name in the criminal hangouts of P.V. His mood kept deteriorating. He got drunker and would not go away. He told us that Mexico's attitude toward marijuana was very liberal. His private attitude was, too, though he never used drugs himself, no, no, no. Did we know that we were entitled to keep some marijuana for our own personal use? Quite a generous amount. I have come to recognize the phrase "your own personal use" employed in a tone of good-natured tolerance as a standard police trap around the world; whatever you admit to possessing is likely to get you put away.

While I let the *federale* buy me drinks, my two companions teased him as though we were all players in *Touch of Evil*. Ken Babbs's Vietnam post-traumatic stress took the form of a dreadful fearlessness, which, though terrifying to timid adventurers like myself, would come in handy more than once. George Walker had a similar spirit. For my part, I went for the persona of one polite but dumb, an attitude that annoyed the agent even more than Babbs's and Walker's transparent mockery. For some inexplicable reason, I thought I could mollify him by talking politics. The agent was an anti-Communist and excitable on the topic. I now realize that in the context of Mexico in 1966 this portended no good. Eventually, having bought every round and rather fumbled his exploratory probe, Agent Number 1 climbed into his Buick and drove off toward Guadalajara. His hateful parting glance told us it was *hasta luego*, not *adios*.

We reported our encounter to Kesey, who was philosophical; he had been brooding, wandering the beach at night. In the morning, he would come down to sleep, exhausted, looking for Faye to lead him to cool and darkness, shelter from the green blaze and the reenactment of creation that could explode at any moment. What was happening to Kesey? He didn't seem to be writing much. It was impossible to tell if we were witnessing a stage of literary development, a personal Gethsemane, or an apotheosis. Some fundamental change seemed to be taking place in the world, and as he smoked the good local herb on the slope of the sierra and watched the lightning flashes and the fires of the volcano, he pondered what his role in it might be. Before his flight to Mexico, he had attended a Unitarian conference at Asilomar, on the California coast, during the course of which a number of people came to believe that he was God. He had spun their minds with unanswerable gnomic challenges and imaginary paradoxes. Still, it was an especially heady compliment, coming from Unitarians. Kesey referred to the Unitarian elders, patrician world citizens in sailor caps and fishermen's sweaters, as "the pipes" because they took their tobacco in hawthorn- and maple-scented meerschaums and used the instruments to punctuate their thoughtful, humane fireside remarks. "If you've got it all together," Kesey asked one confounded elder, "what's that all around it?"

Local adolescents took to hanging out around the Casa. Some of them were musicians. On the anniversary of Mexican independence, we decided to hold what someone called an acid test. People appeared on the beach with rum and firecrackers. We put tricolor Mexican bunting up. By this point, Cassady had found it liberating to restrict his diet to methamphetamine. He went everywhere with Rubiaco, the parrot. So constant was their companionship, so exact was Rubiaco's rendering of Cassady's speech, that without looking it was impossible to tell which of them had come into a room. As for Cassady on amphetamine—he never ate, never slept, and never shut up. He also thought it a merry prank to slip several hundred micrograms of LSD into anything anyone happened to be ingesting. No one dared eat or drink without secure refuge from Neal. To cap off our Independence Day celebration, a number of us went into the village market and bought a suckling piglet for roasting. Nothing roasted ever smelled lovelier to me than that substance-free piggy as we settled under the palms with our paper plates and bottles of Pacifico. We were, unfortunately, deceived. Cassady had shot the creature in vivo with a hype full of LSD, topped off with his choicest methedrine. After two forkfuls of *lechón,* we were bug-eyed, watching the Dance of the Diablitos, every one of us deep in delusion.

How the parrot survived its friendship with Cassady is beyond me; as far as I remember neither he nor anyone else ever fed the bird. Twenty-five years later, on Kesey's farm, Janice and I woke to Neal's voice from the beyond. (The man himself had died by the railroad tracks outside San Miguel de Allende in 1968.) "Fuckin' Denver cops," he muttered bitterly. "They got a grand theft auto. I tell them that ain't my beef." We rose bolt upright and found ourselves staring into Rubiaco's unkindly green eye. If, as some say, parrots live preternaturally long lives, it must be time for some literary zoologist to cop that bird for the University of Texas Library Zoo.

———————

The expatriation had to come to an end; Kesey would have to go back and answer to the state of California. In fact, his spell on the lam had been excellently timed. In 1966, the world, and especially California, was changing fast. The change was actually visible on the streets of San Francisco, at places like the Fillmore and the Avalon Ballroom. Political and social institutions were so lacking in humor and self-confidence that they crumbled at a wisecrack. The *Esquire* consciousness, however, held firm—they declined my copy. "For Christ's sake," an editor kept telling me, "tell it to a neutral reader." They thought I had gone native on the story, and of course I had been pretty native to begin with.

A few months later, Kesey crossed the border and went home. He was able to make a deal for six months at the San Mateo County sheriff's honor farm. No one can call another's prison time easy, but it was less bitter medicine than Cassady's two years at San Quentin. It was also an improvement on five years to life, a standard sentence on the books for a high-profile defendant at the time of Kesey's arrest.

Over the years, my friend Ken became a libertarian shaman. Above all he loved performing; he loved preaching and teaching. He was a wonderful father, a fearless and generous friend, who always took back far less than he gave. Kesey was in love with magic. All his life, he was searching for the philosopher's stone that could return the world to the pure story from which it was made, bypassing syntax and those damn New York publishers. He kept trying to find the message beyond the words, to see the words God had written in fire. He traveled around sometimes, in successors to the old bus, telling stories and putting on improvised shows for crowds of children and adults. If he had chosen to work through his progressively revealed mythology in novels, rather than trying to live it out all at once, he might have become a writer for the age.

Life had given Americans so much by the mid-sixties that we were all a little drunk on possibility. Things were speeding out of control before we could define them. Those of us who cared most deeply about the changes, those who gave their lives to them, were, I think, the most deceived. While we were playing shadow tag in the San Francisco suburbs, other revolutions were counting their chips. Curved, finned, corporate Tomorrowland, as presented at the 1964 world's fair, was over before it began, and we were borne along with it into a future that no one would have recognized, a world that no one could have wanted. Sex, drugs, and death were demystified. The LSD we took as a tonic of psychic liberation turned out to have been developed by CIA researchers as a weapon of the cold war. We had gone to a party in La Honda in 1963 that followed us out the door and into the street and filled the world with funny colors. But the prank was on us.

THIRTEEN

After a spell of thinly subsidized unemployment, it became necessary for me to reach out once more to the world of commerce. I had pretty much had it with hack writing for a while. In the days before the MFA programs spread like Irish monasteries in the Dark Ages, replicating themselves, ordaining and sending forth their novices, aspiring writers often did a measure of hack work, the way farmers inevitably ate a pound or two of dirt every year. A little isn't fatal; if no one did it we wouldn't have our celebrated popular culture.

In moderation, hackery can even be good for you, tune your

ear, provide useful experience and so on. But contrary to what some have said, it's obvious that too much is artistically and spiritually enervating. It seemed to me that a lot of the failed playwrights nursing their cheap cognac through the lobster trick on rewrite at the *N.Y. Daily News* would have been better off if they had never been hired. Anyway, in the name of variation, I thought I'd try for something else. I still had my seaman's ticket but I also had two small children. My wife was trying to raise the kids, attend pre–open admissions City College, and hold a job at the welfare department; for brief periods she was doing all three at once.

Just before our friendship broke up after a bitter quarrel over the Chinese Cultural Revolution, Mike the Mime from the *National Thunder* told me there were guard jobs kicking around at the Museum of Modern Art. Some of his actor friends were doing it. I briefly flashed the image of Mike in the uniform of a Red Guard, with a red-starred cap and a Little Red Book, sternly pacing the gallery in front of *Guernica*. It did seem to me that bug-looking art lovers who couldn't keep their mitts off the Picasso beat waiting tables. I had done a lot of that.

(One day in Calais, Maine, a restaurateur who employed me took me aside to explain that I would never make a waiter. He thought I imparted some kind of strange atmosphere to people's dinner, a fateful tension or pessimism about dinner and life. It was the kind of thing hateful tin-eared people say about my novels, but it was true about my serving style.)

I went down to MoMA to offer my services. The security chief, a man who struck me as surprisingly coplike, was interested in my custodial experience. I told him I had stood shore patrol and served, for a couple of days, at what the Navy calls "prisoner chasing" while awaiting discharge in Norfolk. This was true; the "chasing" consisted of three of us rigged out with clubs and whitewashed spats, SP brassards and .45s, marching court-martial prisoners (CMPs) to breakfast at Camp Allen, the infamous Marine Corps brig. The security chief must have known that sounded more serious and demanding than it was. He remained unimpressed.

What I didn't know, although Mike the Mime, as an honorary Chinese revolutionary, should have known, was that the world was changing fast. MoMA was not hiring posy-picking artists between inspirations. It seemed to want someone who looked as though he could subdue mad canvas slashers and generally keep the stuff on the walls where it belonged. I was out.

On the way to the elevator I chatted with a young woman who worked in the museum offices. She had overheard my rejection.

"Do you know anything about art?" she asked.

"Well, certainly," I told her. "Of course. Me?"

She told me there was a job going as "associate curator" at one of the galleries on Madison. As I would discover, the "associate curator" of an art gallery has duties little different from those of the associate curator of loafers at Thom McAn. So I was hired. In spite of the startling lacunae in my art-appreciation background, I was kept on, mainly, I think, because I could write pay-up-or-else letters that were very polite but quaintly menacing.

The gallery that hired me was what remained of a leftist art collective founded in the thirties that had represented many of the best-known East Coast radical painters. It had recently come under the ownership of one of the founder's relatives, a droll, good-natured man who had spent years in the glass business and who kept a cool and humorous perspective on both art and politics. Neither engaged him passionately, which is not to say he was indifferent or uninformed about them. In fact, having coexisted a little uneasily with two underemployed political fanatics at the *National Thunder,* I had approached this scene with hesitation.

I was surprised to find most of the work at the gallery very conservative, even decorous. There was a lot of romantic realism: young ballerinas *en pointe,* downright Brueghelesque central European villagers ring-dancing in some sweet not so very long ago. There were many sentimental portraits. The political dimension seemed to consist of a commitment to the figurative. The word that suggested itself was "humanist."

Another school of the same movement was also represented. Some of the most arresting paintings were the candy-colored agitprop social satires, cartoonish and sometimes the work of actual cartoonists. These were busy and predictable and seemed guided by conventions, a vocabulary of icons and symbols and instant narratives like those governing early Renaissance religious art. Later I found that many of our artists and their customers, the collectors and supporters, valued orthodoxy for its own sake and looked for authoritative direction. Some of them attacked "art for art's sake," citing fifteenth-century religious art to show the inescapable nature of ideology.

One regular contributor to the gallery had spent the late depression years doing post offices around the country and had a lot of stories to tell. His paintings still looked like studies for murals, a combination of Mexican revolutionary art and postwar Picasso. Somehow the work of this ex-muralist stays with me; he might have been the best of the bunch in terms of talent and the use of it. Also I liked his unself-conscious eccentricity. He wore suits so cheap looking you'd swear they were made in Russia; the sleeves looked like clownish tearaways that would fall off if you shook his hand too hard. He also gave the impression of having his hair cut in Smolensk.

The gallery represented the Old Left pretty much in repose. The McCarthy years had less effect on painting and sculpture than on other arts, except perhaps in museum sales. Many radicals were driven out of their professions, but the artists of our gallery and their sympathizing customers seemed to have survived to live well on the east bank of the Hudson River. It was there, I suppose for the beauty of the place, that they tended to make their homes.

The gallery, in its most engagé period during the thirties, had not catered to the unaffiliated Left. There was pressure from many of the artists not to show the work of anyone whose work the Party did not approve. During the openings, when artists and art lovers reminisced, they tended to boast about their orthodoxy. Earl Browder's dismissal from the American politburo put the kibosh on the Yankee Doodle fife-and-drum Americanism of the Popular Front, and all the art that went with it. Gathering dust downstairs we had scores of Paul Bunyans and John Henrys and Johnny Appleseeds. When Browder fell, and Zhdanov, in Moscow, became Stalin's arbiter elegantiarum, all that bourgeois chauvinism went down with him.

Much of this I learned at the cocktail parties that attended the gallery openings; regulars reminded each other that they had never fallen for Bukharin and certainly never fallen for the unnameable archfiend, the Zionist crypto-Nazi and agent of the mikado, for whom the ice pick was too good. Jay Lovestone had never fooled them for a minute, and they had never thought much of Browder. Khrushchev had given a secret speech, it was whispered, but that might have been disinformation. A few years before, some of the gallery artists and customers had left for the Soviet Union, Mexico, or Western Europe. A fascist coup from Washington was rumored, to be followed by a preemptive strike against the Soviet Union. This treacherous capitalist attack would fail; the agents of the people were on guard for peace everywhere. America would suffer for its designs.

I had always been interested in politics. Belief fascinated me, because of my own experience of lost faith. But somehow, as I lived along with the century, the more interested in politics I became, the further I moved from accepting any kind of transforming ideology as an answer to my fundamental questions. I was never able to advance (if that's the word) beyond the old boring liberalism of the two-cheers-for-democracy sort. Like most people, I never trusted anyone who offered a formula that transcended the instincts of ordinary decency. Ordinary decency, I thought, was about the best of which I, and again most people, were capable. And it was not so easy at that, not so ordinary.

During the sixties and seventies, many people close to my heart, people whom I deeply loved and respected, thought they recognized truth in different political formulas of the Left. Since people who believe they have encountered Truth, no less, call failure to recognize their salvific doctrines "cynicism," I became sensitive to the charge. I insisted during that time that it wasn't true of me. Nor is it now.

Religion was more the thing for me, if only I'd had the sense of humor and good sportsmanship to believe in any. It's reported that Flannery O'Connor and Mary McCarthy once fell to talking about their common background in Irish Catholicism. In fact, it was damn little these two shared. But they had both made their First Holy Communions, receiving the Body and Blood of Our Lord, at different extremities of America. So they discussed the Eucharist, which Mary McCarthy offered was a fine metaphor.

"If it's a metaphor," said Miss O'Connor, "the hell with it."

Blazing, blinding faith, that is. The faith itself had to be something real; it could measurably inform O'Connor stories such as "A

Good Man Is Hard to Find." But there was also something barren about it, something that reduced the infinite variety of the world to a spare grim narrative of human sacrifice. It was admirable in its humility, most of all. But the other side of it, the corps of aggressive know-it-alls who alone had the right to give the orders, was repulsive even at a distance. Later, encountering late-twentieth-century Marxism-Leninism, in the Socialist bloc, I knew it was not for me.

Gatherings at openings drew a few progressive celebrities, but most of the attendees were old-timers. The gallery in the sixties was in a curious political and artistic backwater. But forces were stirring in the larger world, beyond Fifty-seventh Street, beyond Croton-on-Hudson. The intensity of the cold war was fading, and the "paranoia" of the fifties was falling into disrepute among the younger educated classes. Also, by the mid-sixties, the failures in Vietnam were evident. The prestige of America was declining; its heroic role as slayer of police states was being questioned.

The other important empowering force that was restoring militancy came from the civil rights demonstrations in the American South. Our gallery was a little piece of time past. Some of the Party old-timers were encouraged by what they saw as a rallying of the Left on the horizon. Others found the new political activism uneasy-making, druggy, unproletarian, and generally *nyekulturny*. But it was an interesting place to be in the mid-sixties.

The gallery sometimes hired a part-timer for the big opening parties. It was always the same chap, a tweedy, sad Ivy League type. He had been young, gay, and substance abusive when all of these things were attached to penalties. At the openings, I was in charge of the booze, and I usually managed to help myself to a few shots before serving the company. G., the temp, would sometimes take Antabuse and then drink alcohol behind it. This would make him sick, and we would make him space among the frames where he could recline with wet cloths full of ice.

One time, out among the guests, I recognized an old acquaintance. Our encounter partook of absurdity, even absurdism. Getting the next tray of drinks, I had to share this recognition with G.

"You know who's out there? Alger Hiss."

G. was unsurprised. "Yeah. He comes in a lot. He collects."

"Political art? No kidding."

"He likes political art. He was radicalized when he lost his job. At least that's what he says. Oh, and he's gay."

I went back out with drinks. Mr. Hiss was holding forth, talking to two salty old ladies, Party toughies from the days of Youngstown and Seattle. They were laughing at the things he said. I couldn't hear them.

He had a drink in his hand, and he looked not at all like Willy Loman or the American Dreyfus. His expression was what would be called arch, or saturnine. He looked like a Quaker, I thought, old-stock American, purse-lipped, fluty-nosed, with cupid-bowed eyebrows supporting a righteous high forehead. Like a Quaker who was virtuous and sly.

"Do you know him?" I asked G., back in the frame room.

G. smiled and shook his head. He didn't know Alger Hiss to talk to.

Later, I found out that Hiss had done some really good things in the Agriculture Department, gotten the government to pay farm subsidies directly to poor sharecroppers and not just to landowners whose tenants they were. Next time I see him, I thought when I discovered that, I'll have something cool to say to him. But we never met again.

FOURTEEN

The day *A Hall of Mirrors* was published in New York I put in a couple of hours at the gallery, signed for my last unemployment check, and went to lunch at the Algonquin. Candida Donadio, my sainted agent, was with me. Joyce Hartman joined us to represent Houghton Mifflin, my publisher. The book had generous reviews. One, in the Sunday *New York Times,* came from Ivan Gold, whose collection *Nickel Miseries* was the defining fiction of the postwar occupation Army. Another favorable notice was from Granville Hicks. I received an encouraging letter from Joyce Carol Oates that put me on the moon.

It was time for me to face the second book's necessities, although I had nothing quite as substantial as a second book in mind. George Rhoads, a painter whose work I'd managed to place in the gallery over the objections of some of the comrades, told me not to worry. I'd written a book, George said. Maybe it was time for me to do something else. Learn a trade, maybe go to veterinary school or take up oil geology. George himself was at that time a Scientologist, one of those whose careers were supported by infinite time lines and innumerable lifetimes. He could have been a court painter in one incarnation, a gondolier in the next. I knew perfectly well I had one life to squander, that there was nothing other than writing that I wanted to do, nothing else useful that I could do reasonably well. I knew there would be another attempt, at any price. But where to begin?

When *A Hall of Mirrors* was published in London by Bodley Head, in 1968, we went over there, figuring to spend a few months. When work is due but not being done, writers are subject to fits of compulsive motion. To sustain an illusion of progress, any idle journeying or pointless change of circumstance will serve. That writers change publishers, agents, spouses, to dull the nerve that throbs when work stays unwritten is well known. Writers also change cities. Subject to this fidgeting, I now realize, I very nearly changed my life and fortune beyond all recognition or hope of deliverance.

We rented a flat in Hampstead. Its dining-room windows faced southeast, commanding a view down Haverstock Hill, over Kentish Town, Islington, and beyond. By night, our view presented a socioeconomic chart of north London. The streetlamps lighting the hilly terraces glowed phosphorescent white. Down on the flats, the lights burned the color of red lead, refracted in the mist and reflected on the pavements, lowering and brightening the sky to a sort of institutional brick color.

Our rent was reasonable; it was a time when London was still less expensive than New York. We were half a block from Hampstead Heath, and our kids learned to ride their bikes there. Most evenings, at about half past nine, six of us or so, Britons and American expatriates, got together and talked about the things we ought to be doing.

Every few months we would go to north Wales to the house of our friends Jeremy and Eleanor Brooks. Eleanor was a painter, doing landscapes and portraits that gave nothing away to the work I'd been seeing in New York. Her special dedication was and remains to the mountains and forests of Gwyneth, in north Wales; her works in oils and watercolors are among the most beautiful things I own. Her work has been shown in museums all over Britain and on the Continent as well. Jeremy was a novelist and playwright, and later a collaborator with the Russianist Kitty Hunter-Blair on some highly successful translations of Gorky that ran in the West End. He was for some years during our time in London the literary manager of the Royal Shakespeare Company.

We gathered and talked about what we were doing and what we wanted to do. A group of Britons, Americans, Australians, colonials of varying sorts, South Africans, Israelis, Irish, we drank and sought the same refuges to which we'd fled in California. A relentless conspiracy theorist we knew, more than a collector—a connoisseur—justified his exquisite assembly of plots, plans, and stratagems by getting himself registered as one of England's tiny band of marijuana addicts, a brave happy few, resurrected from the shades of De Quincey or Fitzhugh Ludlow, whose condition entitled them to a legal measure of bottled tincture of cannabis—this to be provided by prescription, courtesy of the Ministry of Health. It was lovely stuff; the bottle was true bottle green, "just," as he lyrically put it, "like a carrion fly's ass." A touch to the gum with the little glass pestle in the vessel and presto—hours of profound visual and psychic confusion. Filling a prescription was good for hours of talking shop with fellow devotees at Boots Pharmacy Ltd., Piccadilly, the sanctum sanctorum in London of psychopharmacology. In retrospect, perhaps we had lost our way.

But it was not time wasted. One of our London friends was the expatriate songwriter Fran Landesman, who wrote "Spring Can Really Hang You Up the Most," a hip rendering of Eliot's "Gerontion" that crowns many a cabaret act's closing encore in every time zone from Ronnie Scott's to the Cafe No Problem in Phnom Penh. She and her husband, the writer Jay Landesman, were responsible for the 1959 Broadway play called *The Nervous Set.* They then expatriated to London, where they held what must have been one of the hippest literary salons in the world.

When Ken Kesey arrived in London, together with several of the California Hell's Angels, we were able to introduce them to some long-distance admirers, including the Landesmans and the Brookses. Kesey and the Angels wandered the storied British landscape, discovering people and occasions to celebrate: solstices, equinoxes, the Raising and Burning of Viking Boats, Gypsy sacrifices and Gypsy switches, dolmens and Green Hands, crop circles, sibhs, silkies, and witchery and horned men.

One day Kesey and I went down to Savile Row, an odd angle of haberdashery and helter-skelterdom where the disappearing Beatles had their headquarters. Inside the Beatle Building, which I believe was the location of an entity called Apple Corp., there were hoarse whispers about some kind of Prankster-Apple-Beatle amalgam. It seemed a liquidation was being conducted under the appearance of a potlatch, in a welter of flacks, agents, and bimbos, security guards, sadhus, bare-breasted Scottish girls in boots, riveted into their Shetland-hide breeches. There were English Hell's Angels and California ones, a young woman who said she had climbed Annapurna solo, another who claimed she'd been shot in the wrist with a dart gun. People introduced their songs and disappeared forever. Or else were never thereafter to be out of sight or hearing. In other words it was a music-business publicity-happy media circus.

There were many venues and charged sites—after Savile Row, the Round House, after the Round House, the Albert Hall, after that, Stonehenge. Kesey wanted to organize a trip to Egypt with the Grateful Dead. Something kept happening or, more precisely, kept going on, taking its course, as Beckett put it. Tabloids commercial and irregular kept trying to describe it. It might have been summarized as fucking, drug taking, drinking, press agentry, but above all it was not writing—nobody, nothing. Kesey not writing. Brooks not writing. Stone not writing. We were still young enough to enjoy ourselves.

For a while we left the Angels and Kesey in residence at the Hampstead flat. The generosity and good humor of our Redington Road neighbors in accepting our guests (who were themselves most gracious) was one of the great good things we were blessed with in that time.

When things settled down I found a middle ground between writing the second book and not writing it: freelance journalism and the occasional short story. Some of the journalistic pieces were celebrity puffs and travel pieces, but at the same time I was learning to execute the short story, a form for which I had been raised to have a crippling, exaggerated respect. One of the valid criticisms of writing programs as places to write and study is that the pieces taken as exemplars, the canon of Hemingway, Joyce, and so on, are often so magisterial as to be inapproachable. The result can be that the student is dumbstruck by the science he's supposed to be examining. I did begin to write some decent stories in London. Maybe I required the flakiness and time wasting to lose some of the awe with which writing was still surrounded for me. It's hard to make that sound convincing.

I am not a writer who believes that journalistic writing is a way to learn "economy" or of "approaching essentials" or any of the other piously wholesome-sounding simplicities. Journalism does provide some useful exposure to the world and how people go around in it. Some writers take a lot from the distance journalism requires between writer and subject. Speaking for myself, I don't believe I ever learned anything at all, stylistically, from my years of newspaper and magazine pieces. Which is not to say I think they're all without merit. Some I enjoyed very much, and doing them was doing the right thing for a change. The lessons to be learned from writing fiction and nonfiction—the lessons, I mean, to be learned about each from writing the other—consist in learning how to look at them. The best nonfiction writers—John McPhee, for example—create multidimensional characters, and set scenes in dialogue that have their highest accuracy in the reader's recognition of life and speech.

George Orwell, we know, changed minor circumstances in *The Road to Wigan Pier*. Orwell was a journalist of such scruples that he noted the variances in his journals. In fact, his only agenda was the scene itself, the human situation. It was all that could be required of him.

So much can be said about the intersections of life and language, the degree to which language can be made to serve the truth. By the truth I mean unresisted insight, which is what gets us by, which makes one person's life and sufferings comprehensible to another.

We take an experience, or a character, an event, and so to speak we write a poem about it. The experience, the voices and personalities, pass from primary process to language.

If instructors in journalism, editors and so on teach useful short-cuts, they may be earning their salary, but they're no professional help to their writers. If, on the other hand, they insist on vivid and clear description, they are useful guides. I took something from that otherwise unprofitable time.

I might have served art and insight more perfectly if I had thought twice about what lay behind the possibility of movie deals. I was just back from Sweden, where I had been listening to four long-winded U.S. Navy deserters explaining the moral imperatives behind their jumping ship in Japan to protest the Vietnam War, when my London telephone rang. I think there's a tradition that telephone calls from Hollywood come in the middle of the night. I was sitting up in the wintry dawn listening to the tapes I'd made of the sailors in Stockholm when the polite but insistent ring-ring of our battered black telephone sounded. Indeed it was Hollywood on the line. Paul Newman wanted to make a film of *A Hall of Mirrors*. Actually he was not speaking from California but from Westport, Connecticut, where he was between movies. While the sky lightened over the city, I found myself talking what seemed sheer fantasy. Newman proposed to acquire *A Hall of Mirrors* and perform in it as one of the principal characters. His wife, Joanne Woodward, would play another.

The Newmans had always been known for their left-liberalism, and filming *A Hall of Mirrors* was seen by them and everyone connected with the project as a political gesture. In America, both the

Right and the Left were organizing for the period of polarization that lay ahead. The Vietnam War was beginning to sear the edges and seams of America; in fact, our conversation took place just a few months before a major news event of that war—the surprise Communist offensive timed for the Tet New Year's truce, and the politically vital series of battles near South Vietnam's cities.

A Hall of Mirrors is, among other things, a catastrophic love story within a political setting. It's about three white people, two rootless, one perhaps too profoundly rooted in the old soil. Their fortunes are acted out against the background of the struggle over segregation in the Deep South. I had been years working on it. Over those years I had run into many individuals in the saloons of various bohemias with novels-in-progress in tow. One knew with a dismal certainty that these works were bound to fade away in longhand. My foot on the bar rail as I talked away what I should have been writing, I had always secretly believed I was that kind of writer.

In spite of all the grief I ought to have seen coming, I was well pleased at the idea of a film of my novel. Paul Newman and Joanne Woodward were not only the biggest stars in America then, but conscientious and gifted artists, and politically involved. The film would be a labor of love for these two. Serious attention would be guaranteed. As for the pitfalls of Hollywood, of movies, I knew what everyone thought they knew about the picture business. The movies were fun in something of the same way as comic strips. There were exceptions—mainly foreign productions, a few American classics.

These easy attitudes did not deter me. For one thing I had partaken of the current notion that the world was changing. The scales of decadent convention were supposed to be falling away everywhere. Et cetera. A casting-off of convention, self-consciousness, and clichéd attitudes was working out a general liberation. The truth was supposedly emerging in some way, making people free. I like to think I did not believe this as intensely as some of my contemporaries did, but I did believe it to some degree. And I believed it would have its effect on movies.

The tyranny of the unlettered, conservative moguls and the Catholic Legion of Decency, of whom they lived in dread, would wither. Nor was I deterred by the apparent fact that American films of the middle sixties were among the worst ever made. I put this down to the influence of television and hackery, but most of all to the fact that the older generation of American filmmakers were confused by social change and the expectations of their young audience. They simply had not found the range. They were firing blind, trying to get hip. This phase, I assumed, would soon be over. The adaptation of books like mine, scripted by people like me, with the assistance of the best that Hollywood had, was going to change things.

Being in London also had an effect. Hollywood, in between clinkers, was getting by on huge spectacle costume movies, some of which, like *Lawrence of Arabia,* were very good indeed. Although the British film industry as such was still moribund, British actors and technicians, less costly, were at work everywhere. There seemed to be a common culture informing these films, the English theater, and even British television, one less patronizing to audiences.

Movies, I think, don't lend themselves to innovation, but some of what the younger English directors were doing approached it and impressed me considerably. Nicolas Roeg's truly harrowing *Performance,* starring Mick Jagger and James Fox, achieved ultimate cult status. Using these two actors, one apparently a natural, the other equipped with extraordinary range, Roeg used druggy surrealism as verisimilitude to create a picture postcard from what might be called (with a cringe) the harder side of those dear dead London days and nights, as vivid, evocative, and convincing as a head butt to your perforated septum. In the 7-*Up* series, Michael Apted forced a camera beyond its rational limits, into a narrative structure beyond film's most extreme possibilities. These two films alone might rekindle whatever romance anyone might have conducted with movies.

There was a darker dimension. Selling my first book to the movies was going to buy me time to write my second novel—or to put it another way, to not write it. Once again the illusion of action could substitute for the production of fiction. Offered the prospect of writing the screenplay, I accepted without much reflection. I was not above hoping that the screenplay would take us to Hollywood and make us rich.

So over the short days of London winter I wrote the script. It was far too long, as is usual with first script attempts, but I planned to cut it down. Paul Newman himself sent me a telegram in reply to it. He said he liked it very much. They were, it seemed, going to make my worn, wine-stained, scribbled, and pecked pages into a major motion picture.

I was flown to Indiana, where Newman was filming a picture about the Indianapolis 500, along with Joanne Woodward and R. J. Wagner. We hung out and talked about the possibilities. It was heady stuff. I really had not known what to expect from him. I thought his politics pretty agreeable, and I knew he could command his space. This could be misleading, I thought; he might prove to be a swaggering superbo and a hectoring know-it-all. Newman, as I met him, in his forty-fourth year, turned out to be an obviously shy and considerate man, of grace and reserve. I thought there was a lot of the Midwest about him; that emerged years later, I think, when he played Mr. Bridge in the film of Evan Connell Jr.'s novels. The better I got to know him, the more I liked and respected him.

Finally, in winter 1969, I arrived in Los Angeles. I had been there a couple of times before, once to visit someone I knew in Boyle Heights. I remembered walking by the lake out there. The first gang graffito I ever saw was on a palm tree. It was only a number. Illuminated, it seemed like a medieval manuscript. The number, I later learned, was the listing of the law against murder in the state criminal code. I remembered the good, cheap cafeteria on MacArthur Park. The L.A. I was arriving in this time was another story.

The ride from the airport provided, appropriately enough, movielike scenes. It struck me that the nocturnal exterior of the Beverly Hills Hotel, lit green and yellow, seemed familiar in the way that often photographed settings do. I thought I had stumbled on a small truth about movies. Represented in a film, it seemed to me then, the Parthenon in Athens has no greater iconic weight than the Parthenon in Nashville. On a movie screen Shah Jahan's Taj Mahal is no more moving and majestic than Mr. Trump's in Atlantic City. Trump reduces the Taj to kitsch; on a screen a copy of it is elevated to social commentary. It seemed like a truth worth embracing at the time. I was taking it all too seriously.

Another strange process of recognition was the sight of the hotel's midget bellman in his bright buttons, chin strap, and pillbox hat, a figure whom I associated with a call for Philip Morris, and whom I was astonished to see as a real person in adulthood. I mean in my adulthood.

This was all very blissful until I was shown my room, which was distressingly small. I have to say it was nicely decorated and had a window on Sunset, but still, here it was my night of nights, my sort of *Star Is Born* moment, so I thought, and I was presented by this sinister movie-German porter with a closet. I was cool; I behaved as though, like all the in-crowd, I knew perfectly well the secret of the Beverly Hills, which was that all the rooms were six by eight and that was what the midget in the lobby signified. I hastened to over-tip Gerhart Eisler for carrying my bag and for not spitting directly in my face.

Waking up the next morning I tried to make it come out okay, that, as Alice said, there was plenty of room. Still, there wasn't. I couldn't for the longest time imagine what honor required. To call up and complain about the size of my room somehow seemed tri-fling, effete, absurdly self-important. At other times, not to do it seemed timid, overborne, supine. I decided, with no great confidence in my decision, to complain. When it seemed that no response was forthcoming from the management, I called Coleytown Productions, Paul Newman's company at the Paramount lot. I felt humiliated in two dimensions. Anyway, speaking with John Foreman, Coleytown's producer, I let it be known that I was addressing him from a tangerine-tinted little-ease. With great courtesy he drove over, and I was extremely relieved to see that he was shocked.

"I didn't know they had rooms like these," John said.

However, they had them for me. I changed rooms, then rented a car and drove around with no sense of quite where to go. There was an office for me on the Paramount lot where I could work on rewrites of my script, but before setting out on the changes, I had a long se-ries of planning conversations with Paul, with John Foreman, and with the director, Stuart Rosenberg, whom they had chosen for *A Hall of Mirrors,* aka *Untitled.* (Actually, *Untitled* seems in retrospect rather a better title than any of the other monikers pinned on it at different times. *Untitled,* conjuring up the image of a late Garbo silent, the story of a woman who traded a coronet for a doomed love.)

I didn't have to talk to Stuart very long to find out that we had very little in common in terms of the stories we wanted to tell the world. Our relations were cordial. I was thirty years old; I had always looked younger and, I guess, gave the appearance of a not very with-it graduate student. Hitchhiking through the South, in the days when the roads could be dangerous to outlanders, I had worked up an invisibility suit which enabled me to disappear like a squid in threatening situations. It was a Fisher Body cap, a blue work shirt over a white undershirt, jeans, and Sears work boots. In Movieland I was wary, and I tended to wear the outfit I'd worn in Mississippi. If it didn't transform me into an outright comic yokel, it did give me a distinctly out-of-town quality that would have been spotted and mocked by Nathanael West.

To my astonishment, a full-scale reproduction of the house Janice and I had lived in on St. Philip Street in New Orleans was being constructed on a Paramount soundstage. It was a very peculiar frisson. Somehow I knew it augured bad luck. My favorite recollection about Paramount was that immediately outside its Spanish grillwork gates, on Western Avenue, was a Mexican restaurant called Oblath's, which had what I remember as wonderful food and terrific margaritas. I would spend some of my long expensive afternoon drinking the margaritas, and then walk over to the soundstage where the interior patio of 612 St. Philip was standing. One time, after incidental production had started, I strolled over to find an assistant director supervising two grips who were provoking a catfight. Each grip held a cat, and at the signal "Action!" each would toss his tom at the other. There would be yowling and hissing, but one cat would always chicken out too fast. I stood watching the stunt kitties guided to their marks for take after take. I was still stunned at the sight of my reanimated house. Finally, the AD asked me who I was, and the nature of my business. He had apparently taken me for a geek saboteur from the Friends of Cats.

I moved into the Chateau Marmont Hotel, which in those days was extremely trendy but a little run down, with kitchenettes in every minisuite but no restaurant or bar. Part of the trendiness was its popularity with European film actors of that era who could be seen daily in the elevator, the likes of Maximilian Schell, Jean-Louis Trintignant, Elke Sommer. I remember sharing it once with the English actress Susannah York, who seemed barely upright and as beautiful as anyone could ever be. Having made the polar nonstop from London several times, I always thought it odd that the Chateau was such a preferred destination for Europeans, since the long flight could arrive at any hour and the hotel had nowhere to eat or buy a drink. It does actually resemble a chateau, and is very luxurious and elegant now, complete with catering.

Over my first weeks in Hollywood, shuttling between the Chateau on Sunset and the Paramount lot, I occupied myself with work. My local geography consisted of the director Stuart Rosenberg's house, bounded like Kipling's British Empire by Palm and Pine; a couple of bars; a club that Paul Newman and some of his friends owned; and the Newmans' house up Benedict Canyon. So I was somewhat "in," as they say, and also raggedly lonely. Janice was still in London. She was waiting for the end of the children's school term before bringing them to California. What's more, I kept having these curious contretemps with technicians and other various movie professionals. Why was this constantly happening to me? Was it my simple expression and country face? Of course it was patent delusion on my part to take any of this personally. But I had not forgotten Highspire.

We were all logrolling down the rapids of the nineteen sixties, a broil which, as often as it has been analyzed and derived, retains some of its ineffability. Anyone paying attention in those days remembers institutions that had seemed immune to public pressure appearing to give way at an angry cry from the street. Responsibility was demanded from quarters that had hitherto answered to no one, "empowerments," statutory or otherwise, of all kinds were defined and appeared about to be enforced. Nearly fatal crises of corporate culture suddenly struck outfits such as IBM and the Detroit carmakers, threatening their dominance, and even their survival. The quaintness of Japanese industrial traditions all at once seemed less otherworldly. On the other hand, the annoying eccentricity of the high-tech start-ups in northern California offered competition that had a faintly extraterrestrial quality. And always, Vietnam, engendering between elements of the population hatred not seen in America for a hundred years. Could all these phenomena be somehow connected? Nothing personal.

Organizational and technical changes in movies and television coincided with or perhaps reflected social changes on the street. The many long-haired kids from all over, who had been showing up in San Francisco, appeared now in Los Angeles. California city streets were landscapes I never learned to read, but even to a New York person like myself, the similarities between Los Angeles and San Francisco seemed superficial.

For decades, wandering youths had been showing up in L.A., headed, as they thought, for Movieland. The infantile association of the place with fun was of course a commercial delusion. Money and sex and privilege were brandished. Maybe they were less securely enjoyed there than anywhere else in America. Bohemian style, or an imitation of it, was not much admired. People worked hard, hustled hard, and stole just as they did anywhere else, but the stakes seemed higher. And the place had a culture of predation all its own. It was not a city one went to to find friends, and to abandon precaution there was folly.

The changes hit the longtime steady employees of the studio system harder than they did people at the top. Everything from experimental lighting to scatalogical language and "adult" themes annoyed the technicians and secretaries at the reorganizing studios. At the same time, liberation from the failing grip of the censors did not seem to be making pictures any better. In fact, it seemed increasingly permissible to trivialize on a more complex level, and to employ obviousness in treating stories whose point was their ambiguity. A self-conscious, uneasy world became more so. I was having some anxiety about the transition of *A Hall of Mirrors* to film. I had my alibis early, and by God I'm sticking to them.

FIFTEEN

Janice and the children arrived at last, and in the summer of 1969 we left Hollywood to spend some time in Palo Alto. The revolution was in progress—there were spray-painted slogans on Dinkelspiel Auditorium and broken glass in the fountains. My closest friends seemed all in various ways involved with Maoism, as trade union lawyers, as therapists, and in other socially activist endeavors. No visible improvements seemed to be coming out of this, but it was good to see our friends again. Kesey had been to jail and was now living on the family farm in Oregon, still pondering cultural moves, while raising his kids and pursuing the life of a dairy farmer, somewhat. Our main daily chore while visiting him up in Springfield was an activity known as moving the water. This consisted of carrying and reconnecting the irrigation pipes that made the grazing fields green for the dairy herd. Somehow we spun it into an all-day endeavor. One day a biker came up the road in a dusty uniform with earflaps and goggles like a time-traveling dispatch rider from the Marne. Opening one of his bulging saddlebags, he removed two tiny packets of heroin and presented them with martial éclat. Then he saluted, climbed back on his bike, and headed north. We passed some time snorting it.

During that summer, while the Vietnam War was settling into its second or third stalemate, the first manned moonshot was scheduled to take place, followed by the first moonwalk. It was as though a desperate attempt to keep things positive was being directed from somewhere on high.

At the same time, without any intention of reflecting activities on the moon, three of us set out on a walk across a piece of the earth. Peter ran a bookstore in Santa Cruz, Jim would one day be a judge when appointed by Jerry Brown, and I was a one-book novelist with a shaky future in the movies. Our objective was to walk from Big Sur on the coast south of Monterey inland across the Santa Cruz Mountains. We would go into the mountains at Big Sur State Park and cross the coast range to the Zen monastery at Tassajara Hot Springs. Checking into the park, we were told by the ranger that there were supposedly some panthers and bears in the park, but the only animals likely to give us trouble were the wild boars. Tassajara boars, they were called, and were descended, some said, from local wild pigs, feral Appalachian hogs, and boars imported from Siberia to improve the breed, back when the forest was owned by a British paper company and young executives posted out missed the pig sticking.

"They'll chew their way right up your leg if you get in their way," one ranger said. It made a vivid picture. The ranger may have been chewing our leg, but there was nothing very amusing about what was coming in over the park's police radio as we signed in at the west entrance. It was a description of two fugitives who were somewhere in the park confines.

"All officers alert campers and use caution," the radio crackled. "Whereabouts thought to be in park's north quadrant according to last sighting but present exact location undetermined. One of these individuals is a heavyset male in a lumber jacket with shoulder-length hair. He is known to be armed with a high-caliber rifle and probably a sidearm. The second individual is also known to be armed and has resisted officers, firing a weapon. The second one, slight, dark-haired, seems to be wearing a complete German uniform."

I guess it was the complete German uniform that got to us. Complete! Like this was one gung ho, regulation Nazi trooper! The rangers made no comment as this distressing broadcast came over the wireless. Outside, the loveliest of northern California midmornings was in progress. Beyond the cypresses far below us the blue Pacific rolled.

Our first camp was at the foot of the westernmost front of the Coast Range, near a narrow falls and a forking of the Big Sur River. It was a popular campsite with good water, roughly a day's hike from Highway 1, and made a nice overnight. Beyond the falls, the redwood forest thinned out and gave way to sunbaked fields of tule and live oak, punctuated by granite boulders that centuries of earthquakes had set rolling down from the sierra or beyond. They were the pieces of a jigsaw puzzle whose match might lie on the far side of the Continental Divide.

The trail was dusty, and its muddied spots showed more hoof-prints than backpackers' traces. Big, mean western jays squawked above anything that came along, arresting our attention and mounting regular reconnaissance dives to check our packs for edibles. The ground around the tangled live oak roots was covered with oak balls, the giant fungoid fruit that fell from among the trees' tough prickly boughs. These oak balls were a staple of the wild boars' diet, and where they had worked their way into the earth the pigs would dig them out with their tusks. The Tassajara boar was said to be sizable, but the distance between the gouges in the earth that marked working range of their tusks bespoke animals larger than pigs should be.

On this night of the moonwalk, the overnight campsites near the falls were nearly full, but there was nothing like wonderment or celebration or bring the kids and so on. The prevailing mood seemed a little distressed, as though the pilgrims had gathered in protest against the expedition; there was plenty of protest available. The moon rose late, to mixed reactions along the river. There might have been a ragged cheer. There were definitely some groans and catcalls at the now globalized, industrialized, Americanized moon, once fair. People in whose personal plans the moon might once have played a role were probably upset. Others were outraged at anyone's heckling the moon. There were fights, marijuana smoke. It could make you think of statehood election night in the California goldfields, but no shots were fired.

A wholesome-looking young programmer, who an hour before had been showing me his diver's watch, now accused me of stealing it. He was very stubborn and would not go away; he also had the habit of resting a hand on his sheathed Dacor diver's knife like a hot-headed courtier from Verona. Represented by counsel, our friend Jim, we had to insist to him that we felt unable to let him search our possessions or allow him to assault us. He cried with rage for his lost watch. Radios carried intermittent communications between the surface of the moon and Houston or somewhere. A network rapporteur tried to coax the astronauts a little toward poetry to honor the historicity to which we were witness. An officer who had orbited earlier tried to help him out.

"With your closer visual contact, Howard, she looks like a big bowl of plaster."

Some people found the astronaut's diction sexist and anthropocentric. Later in the night the half sphere showed a ring, reflecting the ocean damp, maybe signaling its violation. If you jammed your face deep into your sleeping bag, you could almost hear the clink and rattle of the astronauts deploying their krypton tripods and gravity-adjusted calipers. We kept our heads down; we were afraid of what we might see—the flash of a logo or, just for a moment, the Goodyear blimp.

Good night, moon.

But many watched, I know, from that forest of redwoods and evergreen oaks, on what they call Piva Dome. Monks, pigs, infantile programmers, poets. The Freikorps Kalifornia Bruderschaft was watching, the Manson Family. They were all out there, I happen to know—all real, every bit as real as Sister Moon, if more transient.

Was that the night that brought forth the line "one small step for man, one giant leap for mankind"? Or was that another time? Jim and Peter and I discuss this sometimes looking back, as we do now. It has become our countermarch, our earthwalk.

The next day we left the company of the river and began a series of climbs and descents to follow the trail inland. The topography of the overland route changes as the walker moves toward or away from the sea. The changes are predictable. In the valleys between ranges there are shadowy groves and redwoods, some of them watered with streams that run low or dry up in midsummer. In the deepest groves, where ferns carry the smell of a sunken river, there are mushrooms so savagely menacing in their ghastly shades and shapes that you can sense the drive to eat them and challenge their poison dreams, and somehow elude their long slow introduction to death. Some of the most spectacular are supposed to be *Amanita muscaria,* the good mushrooms that the guides call "semipoisonous," the psychedelics. There are certainly false amanitas and other killers, equally psychedelic and probably rich in awful insights. Cooking fires were restricted in the summer of '69, the needles and manzanita so dry and bristling you could almost hear them crackle in the night.

Neither we nor, I think, anyone else needed a tent that summer; the nights were cloudless like the days, prodigiously starry, sometimes cold. We had taken to thinking of the sky beyond the tips of the pines as an industrial landscape; we awakened to the drone of jets leaving lacy starlit trails, the twinkling of satellites, all the action and rapine we could imagine on the moon. But sometimes the silence and enormousness of the night horizon made us feel we ourselves might have been in some quarter of the sky.

Mosquitoes varied in size, savagery, persistence. One afternoon we arrived at the creek in late afternoon after an incredibly hot crossing of mesquite uplands. We stripped our backs, fell into the almost still creek, and nearly passed out. Within an hour we were being devoured. This is not hyperbole and it did not involve mosquitoes. Beetles, your cute little ladybugs, covered us completely from our hair to our socks, and the fiendish things were biting us like marabunta ants. It hurt! We were blinded! It took us three-quarters of an hour to scrape them up and destroy them, and they left us with a foul rash. They're nice when it's just a few of them. Phloop, fly away home. But get them on top, in huge numbers, they're not so nice anymore. Biological nature, ontogeny recapitulating phylogeny. Or as William Burroughs used to say: "Insect laughter. Disgust you to see it."

The topography of the coastal mountains repeated itself, changing with the closeness and direction of the ocean and the shifting light of day. In the morning we would break camp and start up the trail through the redwoods. The big evergreens covered the seaboard slopes. As we climbed the lower ridges, there would be meadows and more tule grass, and the live oaks where the boars liked to feed. It grew hot with midday and you would miss the shade but still inhale the fragrance of hot pine from the outboard canyons. Around the rocky canyons overhead, raptors rode the updrafts.

We were on the second day out, happy to have seen no fellow humans. It's hard not to recall that observation about the pleasing prospects and only man being vile. All at once a troop of enormous pigs came galloping across the far margin of a meadow headed toward us on our side of a slow stream. They came fast, looking like cavalrymen following a guidon. We stopped, and a minute later they did. As though at a command, to a silent trumpet and the flourish of invisible banners, they crossed the stream, splashing, it seemed in columns. In long, deep strides they charged—truly charged—across. A rear guard covered the retreat and fell in behind, and they were gone.

The mountaintops, above the shore-facing redwoods on the west slopes and the baked grass and live oaks inland, were treeless except for shrubs, manzanita, and creosote. The going was hard in the absence of shade, and the rocks on the trail were favored in the afternoon by rattlesnakes. We thought about the snakes a lot but never saw or heard one.

On our third day out we came to the edge of the monastery garden. We made ourselves known and went to the Tassajara stream to take our boots off and cool our blistered cankered feet. The stream was intermittently warmed by hot springs and offered any temperature a bather required, from alpine ice to near boiling. Tame trout in the moderate reaches provided restorative nibbling.

It was possible to arise at four and sit *zazen* for the predawn hours. Every day we resolved to do it. It would be pretty to say we did.

After a few days Janice picked us up at the end of the dirt road that came up from the Monterey Valley. Descending the valley's corkscrew road we passed the gilded scions of old San Francisco money, cowboys and cowgirls, hunting boar from the saddle in the golden late afternoon. Servants in white toques piled logs and mesquite for the chuckwagon fires. Scraped gutted boars were hung close by. In those days we knew how oak-fed, fresh, mesquite-smoked boar tasted and made you feel. Like gold honey, like caressing cool flesh in warm silk, the smoky turns of love's canyons, youth and wine. Was it really that good? One of Dante's condemned has a line about remembering in sorrow the days of joy, the worst, he says, of punishments. I no longer remember the taste of slaughtered boar, only recall, now and then, the woodsmoke. The better for me.

———————

After a week or so the moon looked the way it always had, and took the same shapes, and we hardly noticed it. And we were back in Hollywood, where you could have any kind of moon, indoor or outdoor, you desired. That summer of the moonwalk, the estrangement of Los Angeles from itself continued. Locals complained about all the kids. The boulevards were crowded with young panhandlers. There were hundreds of hitchhikers. "Where are they going?" was the jokey question. It *was* puzzling, because they did seem to disappear about where the action ended on the east–west streets. In San Francisco, when the first hippie kids started showing up in the early sixties, local people asked each other, "What do they want here?" It was something of a disingenuous question.

San Franciscans knew their city was attractive. Veterans of the Second World War who'd shipped in and out of its port complex remembered San Francisco with fondness and often wanted to get back. There were many ways in which San Francisco was plainly attractive to the young, and the new arrivals represented many sorts. There was the eternal migration of kids from the country looking for a big city. There were also many urban young, not in search of the cosmopolitan but tired of the slog of New York, which in the sixties was getting increasingly crime-ridden and ugly. San Francisco could seem exotic and certainly somewhat more easygoing. I remember two elderly tourists from New York standing in Union Square, looking about them and saying: "What well-dressed people!" Seems strange now.

Of course there had been Kerouac's *On the Road*. San Francisco also had a reputation for left-wing politics, or at least for tolerating it. The self-satisfied question about what all the migrants wanted reflected fear and irritation, but also the sophisticate's experience that no city could provide the kind of empty transcendence the newly arriving youngsters seemed to be pursuing. San Francisco was just a city, soon to be the third largest in California.

"Where are they going?" was the Angelenos' question about the young thumbing rabble. No one asked, "What do they want here?"

Everyone in the world knew the answer to that. Young girls were coming to be "movie stars," in fact to be prostitutes. The question about their street destination was already an off-color joke. Boys were coming to be some kind of "cooler" people, in significant numbers to be petty criminals, or to escape the rap sheets in their hometowns. Like, wasn't everything you did in Los Angeles like doing it in the movies, or being a character in a rock song? Then there was the lure of sex, surely the biggest illusion of all, since it had long ago been rationed, arbitraged, and factored in L.A., as everything else would one day be.

As expected, like bugs around an electric appliance, the young hopefuls clustered as near to whatever centers they associated with movies, television, and music as they could. As in San Francisco, they learned that they could curry favor with well-off locals by appearing to assume some political attitude or dimension. Protest. The shameless could flaunt their poverty as virtue, like antinomian friars. Not surprisingly, the spirits of the Santa Cruz Mountains were drifting down on the marine layer to contribute their own mystic spookery.

As the filming of *A Hall of Mirrors* (to be released under the title *WUSA*) proceeded, what looked like an alien presence in Hollywood increased. The technicians, the teamsters and grips at the major studios, arrived at work with horror stories about the kids who had appeared on Sunset. They were not like the beatniks down in Venice who knew their place. These kids were dirty, they said, the girls and boys were hustlers, sold drugs. I had no way to judge to what degree these stories were true. Friends of mine would show up in L.A. from time to time and I would give them my version of a studio tour. This always included sullen looks from the film crews.

I had an inner office on the Paramount lot, and an outer office with a secretary. The phone rarely rang. When it did, the secretary would pick up and answer, "Mr. Robert Stone's office." Usually she would be replied to with a wall of stoned giggles and a hang-up.

These calls came from friends of mine, who enjoyed in the frisson of hearing their old pal apparently ensconced in moguldom, on the other side of a secretary who sounded like Irene Dunne.

The project went on location into the New Orleans kind of heat where it was too hot to think. This was just as well for me. For many reasons—principally an utterly unsuccessful attempt to graft one or two (at least two) incompatible elements—the thing in progress slid between incoherency and the nearest equivalent cliché. The novel aspired to a certain poetry and was made of words. The movie *WUSA* came out looking like such a novel rendered as a very indifferent episode of *Matlock*.

There are almost enough unintentional laughs in *WUSA,* the movie to which I myself allegedly reduced *A Hall of Mirrors,* to make its history seem funny even to me. Almost but not quite, considering it provided me with enough regrets to fuel one lifetime's worth of insomnia. Not to mention aggregate hours of boredom and disappointment inflicted as punishment on an innocent audience. All I can say by way of apology is that I suffered too. I should also say that the responsibility for the general badness of it was not the fault of the actors, who worked very hard for a cause we all believed in.

To people who were moved by the book and felt betrayed by the film, I offer my very real regret and my apologies. I felt badly about it, still do. And I suffer with that audience as its numbers grow in tiny increments, year after year, in spongy-carpeted motels in the middle of the night, as relentlessly (but not nearly relentlessly enough for anybody's profit and certainly not enough for mine) the film is shown on television. When I see it go on, I and others like me, who know what happens next, can simply turn it off.

With this in mind, let me take a minute to warn some of the

writers who may later be in the same situation. Remember that as gray dawn finds the last paperback edition of your lovely book, its covers gone, its endpapers (with all the nice quotes from reviews) shredding, the embarrassing movie with which you provided the world (and which all your readers think of as a cop-out) will still be opening for the daily farm report on every functioning television screen at the Parsi-run Motel 6 in Weed, later that afternoon to be watched with increasing incomprehension by the Panamanian maid.

A Hollywood joke of what might be called the "Manson period": You're in Hollywood, you're walking the streets, you've eaten nothing but bananas (what else?) for four days. As you droop at the corner of Hollywood and Vine, a long black limousine pulls up beside you. The door opens: a fat man with short arms emerges. He's wearing a beret and jodhpurs and there's a cigarette holder between his lips. He's definitely in the movies. He's holding a sandwich and he says, "Hey, kid."

Your attention is arrested. The sandwich is a very tasty-looking California sandwich, full of good things, like avocado and watercress. And you know somehow that it's not just nourishment, but maybe . . . a career!

"You want this?" asks the Hollywood man. "It's yours!"

You're so hungry. It's been days. You couldn't face another banana even if you had one. You reach out. You reach out joyfully. Just at the moment when you're about to take it, you notice that, so inconspicuously, on one corner, there's a virtually infinitesimal but unarguably present teeny dab of shit. Naturally you hesitate. You stay your hand, you consider. Then, greedily, you seize the thing. You're thinking: "I'll eat around it."

————

One day everything changed. One afternoon Janice and I were smoking dope with a couple of actors, a married couple, around our age. They were friends of John Wayne's and often appeared in his westerns, and they observed that he would not have approved of their smoking gage.

The wife had been to the beach, where she said she had seen two animals fighting.

"What kind of animals?" I asked her, picturing, I suppose, Kodiak bears or elephant seals.

"I think . . . I think," ventured the stoned lovely, "I think they were winkles."

Everyone watched in leaden-eyed tolerance while I rolled around the fuzzy rug, convulsed. It was the funniest line I had ever heard in my life. Forty minutes later, when I had suppressed my last yak, we went outside to look over Benedict Canyon. It was the kind of Los Angeles summer day that Nathanael West could describe with such exquisitely turned admiration and loathing. Sumptuous, sensual, euphorbia-scented. Hummingbirds sipped nectar.

"That's the house," the young woman who had seen the animals said.

The four of us stood and looked down at an attractive greenswarded property on Cielo Drive in Bel-Air. I had stopped laughing. For quite a while we stood and looked at it. Everyone had to have a look.

I was walking into the coffee shop of the Beverly Hills Hotel the next day, and a couple of women who worked in the gift shop were in close converse. One listened openmouthed and pale. The other, the speaker, said her husband was a deputy and had been to the house. He had seen awful things there and had been unable not to tell her.

"He said it looked like a fag murder," the deputy's wife said.

I filed the line away, never to use it, but her story sort of spoiled my day. I went back to the Chateau to do a joint with Janice.

"Where did you get the dope?" she asked. "Did you buy some?"

It was Jay Sebring's dope, and he had given it to me at a party. Jay Sebring, who had named himself after the Florida seaside raceway, was now dead, a victim of the Mansonites. He had been a hairdresser from New Jersey, had reinvented himself in the Hollywood style, a nice man. He was a friend of Abigail Folger, a woman I knew a little. Abigail was born to ride in pursuit of those boars up in the Carmel Valley, as beautiful a flower of California as grew. Her wealth came from coffee. She was intelligent and kind and as classy as could be. She spent a lot of time volunteering with children in Watts. Many people say they will never forget what she was like, what her smile was like, until the young nonconformists eviscerated her to write misunderstood Beatles lyrics in blood on the wall of the house on Cielo Drive.

It was saturnalia time in Hollywood, a very grim feast of the meaningless. The youngsters disappeared from the boulevard as though the bad father of the feast had eaten them. For some time Manson went uncaught and the police put out false leads. Before his capture, the most extraordinary speculations as to motive and perpetrator went around. The most unsettling involved the number of people who suspected one another of having a hand in the murders. This included *famous* people who used not to do such things.

Then the Manson Family went down, and the theorizing and the interpretation exfoliated. Nixon had done it. Why? To embarrass the antiwar movement. A well-known person offered a theory that naval intelligence had killed the victims, which I personally resented. A droll speculation, that one, because it involved the CNO, old Mormon Admiral Moorer, reviving the Phineas Priesthood and sending forth the assassins, all in the name of victory in Vietnam.

Fear appeared in a handful of dust. When the bearded trolls and their consorts were run out of town, fear remained. People hired bodyguards. At one house (I swear) the protection would follow a swimmer doing laps up and down the length of the swimming pool, admittedly a very long one. One movie person claimed she had fired her security when the man asked if he could come inside and play the piano.

"I'd just as soon . . . you know." Indeed.

Something over five years after the John F. Kennedy assassination, and the event had something of the same resounding emptiness. Hollywood is a self-referential place and then as now it was full of rise and fall and blighted hopes, anger, disappointment, dope, and toadying and jealousy. Everything except maybe good sex. Suddenly something happens that makes everything even less sensible and significant than before, the total nothingness at the heart of thing-ness explodes in front of you. Not everyone's a philosopher. Never did the lights go on so fast and the glitz come off the columns and the glass balls shatter as in the wake of a couple of murders.

Things could not be made to be the same. There was an earth-quake, really—a small one, but we felt it at Oblath's.

A number of people who were friends or acquaintances of Kesey passed through town. Kesey's credo was that nothing human was alien to him, and most folks were close enough. Ken's friends, a wandering band known as the Hog Farm, had coalesced around a cultural figure who called himself Wavy Gravy. Wavy had once been a café poet in New York and had followed the sixties trail to Califor-nia, where some transcendent experience had provided him with a renewed identity and new name. One of the stories current about him was that he had been cashiered from the comedy troupe the Committee for appearing for a show in a tweed jacket with salami arm patches. The Hog Farmers were fine young people for all I ever knew, but it was bruited about that they spent some time out at the Spahn Movie Ranch with the Mansonites. Me, I was a friend of Kesey's, too, a friend of a friend of Richard Baba Ram Dass Alpert, who had bum-tripped me back when. Alpert was the ex-colleague of Timothy Leary, who knew everyone and had connections with the Brotherhood of Eternal Life, who were considered heavy. And connections proliferated. Leary's "archivist" was my NYU and Paris pal Michael, the man who would go on to become the father of a beautiful movie star, although this was naturally unknown at the time. We were smoking Jay Sebring's dope, and so on and so on.

As the summer of 1969 lengthened, there was a whole lot of shaving going on in Los Angeles. Good-humored tolerance of the neo-bohemian scene was suspended, and whatever it was was not funny. Fear inhibited.

———————

We decided to go back to England. Life was sane, sort of, and relatively predictable. Before setting out for London we went to what might be called a farewell party. Nitrous oxide was currently big on the scene. In the nineteenth century, many will know, it played a role in American scientific and intellectual history. At Harvard, the very place Ram Dass and Leary were experimenting with LSD and turning students on to William James, the author of *The Varieties of Religious Experience* and brother of Henry, the brother of the master novelist had conducted his own experiment with nitrous oxide, some eighty-odd years earlier. Nitrous oxide was used early as an anesthetic in dentistry, and Harvard students had taken to frolicking with the stuff. So joyous were the cries of delighted insight that Professor James heard echoing through the Yard that the liberal-minded and adventurous scholar thought he might try some.

One evening the savant set a tank by his bed, connected to a pipe. As the chimes sounded across the gables, Professor James passed into a profound reverie. Suddenly he came to consciousness, his intellection ablaze with discovery. He had happened, with the aid of this wonderful elixir, on the very meaning—but the very meaning!—of life. Pen and ink were at hand. No sooner had he time to write than a second drowsy numbness passed over him. In the morning he awakened to the merry bells. Leaping from his stern scholar's bed, he seized the sheet of paper upon which he had inscribed life's meaning.

This is what he had written:

Hoggamous Higgamous, Man is Polygamous
Higgamous Hoggamous, Woman is Monogamous.

How true! And even the obvious must be reexperienced down the generations. That this wisdom not perish but be found by each age in its time may have been the reason for the sudden very-late-sixties popularity of nitrous oxide.

Another joke of the era:

"Man, can you fix me with a doctor that writes?"

"No, man. But I can put you with a hip dentist."

Anyway, nitrous oxide and its discontents. The party we were attending was indeed a farewell party, since we were bound back to England, now home. But it was, further, a farewell party for the late owner of the nitrous oxide, a graduate student who had delighted in taking his gas while relaxing in a hot bath. While asoak, the luckless man passed out. While he was out, his head slipped beneath the water to rise . . . never.

Farewell, as Poe observes, the very word is like a bell, and Poe and this graduate student I'm certain would have liked each other.

There was a lot of gas left over, which was good because there were a lot of us there. Here I steel myself for confession. Few readers will fail to experience outrage at what I now feel bound to disclose. But if there is a God in heaven—William James would have known it.

All right, our kids were with us. Everybody's kids were with them. So we were doing gas with balloons, and you know how kids are with balloons. I mean you had to be there. It was a beautiful day. The kids were having such fun! There was so much gas. And it was hardly as though the late owner of the gas were lying there drowned in a bathtub; he had passed on, and he certainly didn't require any more gas.

And the kids so liked the balloons, and of course they liked the gas too, taking the gas from the balloons. How this happened, what happened next, nobody is sure because everybody was ripped and fighting greedily over the gas, and the children were fighting greedily over the gas too. So to square it, even-steven it, we declared, we the adult authority, come on, kids, just one balloon's worth to a kid.

When, would you believe, this one little tyke made this snarky face right at me and said ha ha or hee hee or some shit, "These aren't balloons! They're condoms!" And by the spirit of William James, they were condoms. We'd been getting loaded watching small innocent children sucking gas from condoms.

So if the Society for the Prevention of Cruelty to Children had finally caught up with me there, would not the cry have been: Exterminate the brutes!

So we left for London.

SIXTEEN

Years before, circa 1960, while George Rhoads and I were painting apartments on Central Park West, we would play station WBAI so that George could bend his mind's ear over some postmodernist music. Neither of us, frankly, was a great fan of Schoenberg or Berg. George liked mid-twentieth-century music for what he genially called its "creepiness."

The music we painted to was accompaniment to the station's news and commentary. Much of this both George and I, who considered ourselves among the well informed, found abstruse. It amounted to denunciations of American policy in the former

French colonies in Southeast Asia. I was not persuaded. Considering how fond I was of my own opinions at that young age, I ought to have paid more attention.

The subject, it turned out, would persist. And the war. It would be the issue, politically, that dominated a lot of my life. I saw myself as a writer whose work reflected politics, so of course there was literally no escaping it. Too bad you can't pick your history. The degree to which the Vietnam War consumed the vital energy of the nation, degraded the honor of its stand against the hateful ideologies of the twentieth century, and used up the lives of its youth was tragic. Tragic seems a paltry word, but what can one say? The ruin and death we inevitably brought down on Vietnam will always be held against us. It will be recalled as one of the crimes of history. In fact it was worse than a crime; as a coldly wise Frenchman said in another connection, it was a blunder. However, no one now requires more moralizing on that topic.

Yet maybe I just can't stop. Let me say that my tendency to run on is not the outrage of a Vietnam veteran, which I certainly was not. Nor is it that of a committed journalist in the line, because I was not that, either, as was, for example, Michael Herr, who survived Khe Sanh. My role was somewhere between that of a tourist and a writer in residence.

It was the spring of 1971; the war was lost. I had just taught my kids, in London, to ride their two-wheel bicycles. I didn't want to be there, in Vietnam; I didn't want to stay. I didn't want to leave, either, because it seemed betrayal.

Maybe many of those who participated conspicuously in the "debate" are proud of their contributions to it. In my opinion most of them ought not to be. In the time between my discharge from the Navy and the time I went to Nam I remember how the war sidelined so many other concerns that were vital to the country. I remember the crowds of which we were sometimes a part, Janice and I. The Berkeley-Oakland city line, where the Oakland cops let the Hell's Angels attack the demonstrators. The space before the Pentagon, in Washington, D.C. Fifth Avenue and the United Nations, in New York. And Grosvenor Square, in front of the American embassy in London, and Haverstock Hill, site of many antiwar demonstrations. The brandishing of right-mindedness and chauvinism, the surfacing in both America and Europe of hatreds that had little to do, finally, with war in Asia.

In London, I remember my beloveds giving blood for the National Liberation Front. I had a dream once of the blood, huge gouts of it in aluminum containers, being poured into a sewer drain somewhere. Maybe it wasn't a dream, just an inappropriate notion, like that of piety settling like a dirty-smelling film on the furniture.

But this is mellow retrospect. We felt involved. Eventually, the incessant talk, the examinations of consciousness, the doubts about where truth lay became more than I could bear as a distant witness.

When I found that I had arrived, somewhat to my own astonishment and horror, at Ton Son Nhut airport in the spring of 1971, my only experience of war had come as a U.S. Navy sailor in 1956 at Suez, when we had watched the French naval air wing attack the defenses at the harbor at Ismailia, Mystère jets coming in at the top of our radio rig. That had been enough for me. Or so I thought.

But in 1971 I was in London with no second book written and a pretty poor excuse for a movie headed for late-night TV with my name on it. It seemed to me that if I was going to continue doing my job, I had to go over to the country and the struggle that was the center of so much of life's passion. Ed Victor, who had been an editor at Jonathan Cape, together with some associates, was putting together a London weekly tabloid modeled on New York's *Village Voice.* It was called *INK.* I procured a letter from Ed, and one from Mike Zwerin of the *VV* itself, addressed to whomever I found in charge over there. I bought a cheap ticket to Saigon, via charter to Kuala Lumpur, from an Oxford Street bucket shop and took off.

Spending the night in Kuala Lumpur, I had Southeast Asia come upon me. The scent I remember was of incense trees on the way into the city. I spent the night walking the Chinese quarter, intoxicated with jet lag and the street life. Of course this was all more than thirty years ago and Kuala Lumpur did not yet contain the world's highest building. In my meaningless terms, it appeared still lately postcolonial. Let me not say unspoiled.

The next day I flew Air Vietnam to Saigon. At Ton Son Nhut, as I went through customs, an enormous clap of thunder sounded out of a nearly black sky. The many Americans around the civilian terminal stopped what they were doing, tensed, and faced the sound.

I checked into a hotel called the Royale on a street called Nguyen Hue, a place suggested by friends in London. It was the hotel of choice of the "third-country press," meaning many of the European reporters and photographers who were not, as they say, on board. The Royale was inexpensive but wonderfully atmospheric, a quality I was in the market for then. The Americans who stayed there were, in general, not on board either, but extremely knowledgeable. Judy Coburn, who wrote for the *Nation,* was a fellow guest and one of many people there who were of great help to me in finding my way around.

My credentials from *INK,* as it turned out, were not acceptable to the Military Assistance Command, Vietnam: MACV (Mac Vee, like some Scots Covenanter or hairy-handed Irish chief). My press accreditation was to the Vietnamese Ministry of Information, which entitled me to the courtesies and cooperation—in matters like transportation—of the ARVN, the Army of the Republic of Vietnam, what GIs called the Arvin. The courtesy was more than satisfactory. The transportation, I was told, was less than reliable. Also, like most reporters, I was inducted into the Arvin with the honorary rank of major. I was given a pin with the little curlicue of a French major's epaulets to sew on my uniform, if I had owned one.

I found it possible, for the most part, to insinuate myself into the American presence and talk my way aboard such vehicles as I might require to travel wherever I might want to go. Once, the Marines laid on a press pool helicopter to Da Nang, and thence to Phu Bai. I got another ride into the mountains to a lonely place called Dakto. There were still some American troops there, and the place was attacked later in the year. In the course of my brief ventures, I learned it was customary to sit on one's flak jacket (borrowed, in my case—my unweathered unmilitary gear attracted attention). Passengers in the choppers sat on their flak jackets to protect themselves from internal injuries in the event of a round from below. People told the story of the guy who spent days in surgery having little pieces of a map removed from his interior spaces. I had a ride from Ton Son Nhut to another beautiful, lonely place called Dalat, a resort once.

At Phu Bai, a longtime Marine base south of Da Nang, at Da Nang itself, at Dakto during the Tet offensive of 1968, and at the citadel of Hue, incredible courage and self-sacrifice were displayed by troops on both sides. But the North Vietnamese Army, briefly in control of Hue, treated the city and its inhabitants the way the special Kommandos of Totenkopf SS treated the average Byelorussian shtetl. When evidence of this was *unearthed,* as they say, the business went a little underreported in Europe and the United States. It roughly coincided with the American massacre of villagers at My

Lai. Since most newspapers are into telling readers what they are used to hearing and think they already know, any suggestion of congruity in the cruelty of desperation would have been the occasion of moral confusion.

In Ayutthaya, Thailand, I chatted with a French businessman named Dur, which I thought was a great name for the sort of tough old colonizer he was. He had been captured by the Communists in Hue and, as a French civilian, spared. The two French Benedictines he was staying with, however, were not spared: one was burned, one buried alive. Before that, Dur had been an officer in the Colonial Naval Infantry attached to some regiments of the Légion Etrangère. He said of the three U.S. Marine battalions who took the Hue citadel, "Listen, I would have kissed these *types,* eh. They fought like legionnaires." In the *poissard* those thuggy old-time Frenchies spoke everyone was *un type.*

Looking around the citadel years later, I held my manhood cheap that I was not there on that Saint Crispin's Day. But I wasn't. I'm grateful I wasn't. I wouldn't have liked it. Back in Ayutthaya, it provoked me to tell M. Dur about Ismailia and the French Navy potshooting the mole. He laughed. He added that even the Arvin troops at the citadel, from which not so much was expected, had fought very well too, because many of their families had been tortured to death during the three weeks of NVA control.

Outside of some ceremonial mortaring from beyond the perimeter, Americans were scantily engaged in the spring of 1971. As for the mortars, the other side had to do something with all the hardware they were collecting from the Russians and the Chinese. But the Nixon regime had already started pulling grunts out of the line. Something called "Vietnamization" was in progress, in which American troops would be replaced by Vietnamese.

Odd things were happening, but I was wanting to go home. Much as I loved the Royale, its colorful, Corsican proprietor and its clientele, I was restless. Restlessness and ignorance led me to entertain a thoroughly dreadful idea. I went over to one of the network offices at Graham Greene's old haunt, the Continental, and asked the guys whether they thought going to Cambodia might be a good idea. I don't know what they thought I meant by that. I don't know what I thought I meant. I'm still puzzled by the enthusiasm with which one network man encouraged me. I was thinking, among other things, of the opium dens I had heard about in Phnom Penh, and the drolleries of the Lon Nol regime, although I didn't mention such things at the Continental. However, the rat from Televisionland really insisted I go for it. I must have seemed to be more of a pain in the ass than I imagined. By then Sean Flynn, Dana Stone, and other adventurers who had ventured across the Parrot's Beak were already dead. A certain playfulness about the network man's tone eventually discouraged me.

Regulars at the Friday Night Follies, the weekly briefing sessions for the press, were receiving relentlessly upbeat reports that they considered less than reliable. I was falling out of touch with the big picture. The more days I spent in the country, the further I felt from anything I could conceive of as a narrative of the war's course.

By this time I had located some kindred spirits and was sliding into a pattern of life that could best be called alienation, in every sense of the word. I was part of the "stringer" world, stringers being the journalistic trade term for part-time or semi-employed or otherwise unattached members of the press. Of itself there is nothing compromising about being a stringer; energetic and courageous stringers in the right place at the right time have been responsible for some great journalistic coups. But I was hanging with some of the less reputable elements in town, regularly visiting a crash pad on Tu Do Street (once the rue Catinat and the home of Givral's ice-cream parlor). The apartments were rented by a gang of mainly Australian photojournalists and writers, and their mainly Vietnamese girlfriends; the odd Filipino or Filipina rock musician might also show up. Anyone, actually, might show up—from an overzealous war protester who had decided to carry her protest to the very edge of the pit, to the editorial staff of a midwestern high school newspaper who had simply applied for a Vietnamese tourist visa—like mine—and taken Daddy's credit card to Thai International Airlines.

Every few days, a number of us might take off out of town toward the huge complex at Long Binh and follow the traffic. One route might take us beyond the Capital Military Zone and a short distance in the direction of what was called the Iron Triangle. This road led to the Michelin rubber plantations and, at Cu Chi, the headquarters of the Twenty-fifth (Tropic Lightning) Division. We never thought of running the whole route overland.

At Cu Chi the army had fought its surreal and truly horrifying war in the tunnel complex that housed the operations of the Viet-cong–North Vietnamese Army contingent responsible for the provinces around Saigon. Farther along the road, the army had fought two operations called Cedar Falls I and II along the edge of the Ho Bo woods. The road ran between rice paddies, dry or flooded, depending on the time of year, and rows of rubber trees. At the jungle terminus was the capital of the Parrot's Beak, Tay Ninh, home of the cathedral of the syncretic Cao Dai sect, whose avatars included Jesus, Buddha, and Victor Hugo. From Tay Ninh a continuation of the road approached An Loc and the border with Cambodia.

In my brief period there, Cu Chi was approachable, and we would go out there on motorbikes, me riding double with a drinking buddy whom I've written about under the name of Harry Lime. By now I've called him Harry Lime for so long that I can't remember his actual name. Nowhere in the country was completely secure at that time, but we were once advised that near the capital, our principal danger might come from encountering a wandering battalion of Korean infantrymen, or else some escapees from one of the Arvin's penal battalions. These were mainly perfectly respectable Vietnamese soldiers being victimized in some fashion by rogue superiors. But resentment was building so late in the failing war.

A section of the tunnel complex at Cu Chi, ostensibly cleared of the enemy presence, had been converted to use by the Twenty-fifth as a tunnel school where infantrymen were instructed in tunnel-fighting tactics against the army that had built the tunnels and had been at home in them since the Japanese occupation. It seemed to me a course of instruction about as useful as a three-week intensive immersion seminar for eternity in hell. EVERYTHING YOU'LL NEED DOWN THERE AND HOW TO USE IT!

Press people in Saigon (and U.S. soldiers stationed there) could choose from a formidable menu of user-friendly processed drug packages. The handiest way to score was to walk to any downtown corner where Vietnamese ladies ("mama-sans," in the U.S. Army occupation-pidgin spoken in Japan) sold American knickknacks of all sorts, usually stolen, or sometimes illegally purchased from PX stores for resale on the street. Among the duty-free Luckies and razor blades, a brand of cigarettes called Park Lane was on sale. Park Lane cigarettes were machine-packaged, filter-tipped marijuana joints. They came twenty to the cardboard packet, in a conservative presentation, complete with crushproof box, cellophane wrapper, and familiar design—not in the least sportive or coy. The marijuana was of indifferent quality. Connoisseurs, of whom the U.S. Army had very many, derided the contents as factory floor sweepings, and street lore said the cigarettes were assembled by lepers.

Joints available at our Tu Do Street repair were of a different order. The concierge there always wanted good-quality American laundry soap. For a family-sized box of detergent she would exchange a packet of well-made joints soaked in opium or clear liquid heroin. Sometimes the additive was brown heroin that bubbled aromatically under the wrapping paper, sidewinding the joint as one held it. But sometimes it was powdery white and sparkled as it burned. There were no geekish additives like acid, angel dust, or cheap speed, later Communist innovations. These, like fake icons and counterfeit American Zippos with backward lettering, came in with Russian sailors.

Vietnamization was cutting down on American military traffic in the Saigon–Ton Son Nhut–Bien Ho conurbation, but there were still enough U.S. armored columns and truck convoys to justify the comfortable existence of a helicopter-borne, on-the-half-hour traffic reporter who could guide his listeners through town. This soldier's nom de guerre was "Parker Lane," and he became a figure of legend. In some versions, Parker shared some general's live-in lotus petal, who got the giggles driving with her boss to the office and confessed all. The brass hat punished Parker with some life-threatening assignment, transferring him, for example, to the Hanoi Traffic Report. In other versions, he thrived.

Anyway, as I did not yet quite realize, I was not over there to be Ernie Pyle or Richard Harding Davis. The story I had was the stuff of fiction, and if I could make it worthy fiction I was quits in the scheme of things. If it distracted my compatriots with a glimmer of the insight by which this race survives, if it served truth, then I had done my job, about as much of an accomplishment as I might hope for, and not nearly so easy as I had imagined. But my time there had been short, and I was among people who despised risk and seeing young men whose early deaths had been imposed on them. (There were young women too, who endured horrible deaths, most of them Vietnamese—NVA or VC nurses, for example, daring Communist cadres, or too-popular Catholic-school teachers.)

In the hands of those screwballs at Palo Alto Stanford Hospital years before, in Antarctica and Ismailia, I had felt ready for anything. Now I wanted to see my kids ride their bicycles. How many times did journalists in the line hear the bitterness of drafted soldiers, risking it all for their buddies, for their personal honor, even—God help us—for their country, as they had been told and believed? How many times did one hear it: You don't have to be here, you're here to make money off it, you could be anywhere you wanted—with your high school and your college—anywhere—but you're here, you sick son of a bitch, here, because you eat this shit up, don't you, and I hope you die, you rotten-hearted motherfucker, I hope you die. Many times.

Because, of course, why should you be alive when his lovely buddy was now a maggoty shitstain riding a black plastic bag, in an overpriced coffin under a flag, in his welcome-home parade? Difficult to answer.

However, as I insist, I had my job and I was doing it. One Friday, prior to crashing a party at the Continental that would celebrate the retirement of a U.S. Air Force general, or else a change of command—something—I crashed the Friday Night Follies. I was merely Major Stone of the South Vietnamese Army without my JUSPAO card, so unauthorized infiltration was necessary. Admission to the Follies turned out to be far less difficult than I had imagined. I felt for the briefers. By this time only hatred of the reporters sustained them. The military may train you at apple-polishing and a little artful dodging, but it doesn't exactly train you to lie. Then again maybe it does.

Other correspondents provided what I considered more reliable information about the course of the war. The most important military operation of the past few months had been an incursion into Laos from a remote province of northwestern South Vietnam.

The U.S. had fortified the decommissioned Marine Corps base at Khe Sanh. This time it was not the Marines as garrison but the Army's famous 101st Airborne, along with a brigade from the Fifth Infantry. The 101s were about the best troops Mac Vee could deploy.

So it was rather high profile for any border jumping. Khe Sanh is still probably the best-known battlefield of the American Indochina war. The most beautiful too, although too few had time to notice. I once had something of an argument over this observation, as though such a declaring of a place where so many died must be a play for irony. No.

Khe Sanh had become famous because of a nearly two-month siege its Marine garrison endured before the Tet offensive of 1968. The base was athwart the Ho Chi Minh Trail, commanding high ground over the Ashau Valley, close to the Laotian border. Because the Communist effort against it was so fierce, because of its position in the northwest corner of South Vietnam, it invited comparisons with Dien Bien Phu, a battlefield to the north where the French had essentially lost Indochina forever.

In late 1967, Khe Sanh's defense had obsessed Lyndon Johnson. He kept repeating his determination that it not become for the United States what that other place, Dien Bien Phu, had been, the place whose name was an infernal bell no Christian could pronounce, where the heathen played poker without cards for no money. His

Texican passes at sounding its tones were a bad Washington in-joke. But it was no joke to him; Khe Sanh was not that goddamn place, nor would it be, because its fall would disgrace the name of Johnson retroactively to the first generation and henceforward. The president ordered a replica of the Khe Sanh base constructed in sand and placed in the White House Situation Room so that he could oversee the fortunes of its defense at any hour. He had ordered the Communist troops investing it subjected to heavy bombing from air bases as far from the scene as North Carolina. People who were there (Michael Herr, for instance) knew that to be there was worse than could be imagined from Washington, and remember it through rings of fire. "Maybe memory distorts," Michael said.

Six months after the siege, by which time the Communists had removed their troops to attack the urban area near the coast, the place was bucolic again. Marine patrols discovered, it is averred, that Communist troops around Khe Sanh had always controlled its water sources and could have closed them off at any time. The month after that, the base was dismantled. Secretly, no announcements.

Khe Sanh was just a mountain, it wasn't going anywhere. Like its lovely companion peak Apbac, which came to be known as the American Slayer, it didn't really command anything except a succession of ghostly, foggy mornings, oblivious of the dead. Years of the morning's fog and the evening's mist rose and fell to the lamenting of wolves turned ghoul and tiger spirits. Evangelical missionaries to the Lao and the Hmong there saw devils.

Nevertheless, in early 1971, the can-do Seabees turned to with their jackhammers and articulated loaders to provide Khe Sanh—now ever so strategic again—with contoured ammo pits and latrines and sheds, with helipads and A-9 landing strips. It was all to be part of the American support effort behind a military operation called Lam Son 719.

With its runways and supply facilities restored, Khe Sanh would function as the forward support area for the American forces. The attack itself, the penetration of the Laotian border, was to involve ARVN ground troops and American air support. Reporters haunting the border, looking for a ride in and a closer look, kept encountering that strange Army-colored stenciled sign that looked so incongruous in the jungle, NO U.S. PERSONNEL BEYOND THIS POINT. There were some officers, though, unwilling to let their Arvins go it completely alone. And there were reporters, at least one press pool, of which I was not a member.

In the U.S. Congress, a law called the Cooper-Church Amendment had been passed, limiting presidential war powers. No funds would be authorized for American expeditions to Cambodia or Laos. General Creighton Abrams wanted very much to interdict supply routes on the Ho Chi Minh Trail inside Laos while the weather was still dry enough to keep them operational. Mac Vee thought, correctly, that the Communists were planning an offensive at the first opportunity. It was hoped Arvin troops might be able to cross the border and close the trail down.

One January midnight, "Lam 719" sent fifteen thousand Arvin troops along Route 9 toward the border of Laos. What happened then is well known. Heavy rains and cloudy skies, arriving early, limited the capacities of American air support. Route 9 inside Laos was slow going in any weather. But the Arvin persevered. Then, for political reasons now obscure, the Arvin field commander was ordered to slow his advance. (Increasingly mired, they lost all the necessary elements—initiative, surprise, confidence.) The skies stayed dark. Gathering around the Arvin positions, the Communists mustered sixty thousand men, as large a concentrated force as they had ever put in the field. Eventually prodded by General Abrams (who apparently made an authorized visit over the border) the Arvin forces reached the Laotian town of Tchepone in March. It had been largely abandoned.

"Take a piss and go home," President Thieu ordered his CO on the scene.

But there was hardly time for a piss. Where the empty muddy street of Tchepone had been, and the ruins of Route 9, sixty thousand North Vietnamese appeared. The debacle was wholesale and horrible. Americans of an age will remember the picture of the Arvin soldier clinging to a medevac helicopter tread as it ascended, desperate to get away.

Other soldiers clung to chopper treads trying to go home. Some pulled the helicopters out of equilibrium, causing them to crash. Some lost their purchase and fell to their deaths. (Some were beaten to death by tree branches, rocks, thorns, pulverized by the forest.)

So it was not a victory this time. The Arvins lost about ten thousand. Even the American air support troops took heavy casualties from North Vietnamese T-35 radar-guided antiaircraft tanks.

The war correspondent François Sully, a longtime veteran of Southeast Asia and a much-decorated former French officer, died there. And Larry Burrows, the great photographer. Of course Khe Sanh and Apbac Peak, Lord of Ashau (Hamburger Hill to us), had to be abandoned. No other American strategic plans were offered in the course of the war, except for the final bombings, Linebacker III. Those in Washington who had so feared the ghost tigers at Khe Sanh, the wolves of Dien Bien Phu, had brought those creatures to their door.

After Lam Son 719, everyone said in Saigon, things changed. One afternoon, it seemed there was going to be a race riot out in front of the old opera house that the example of American democracy had transformed into the National Assembly. Vietnamese in the street seemed to be turning on passing foreigners, foreigners of any kind. Arguments over cab and cyclo fares tended to get physical.

There were rapes in the city of Saigon. To this news the reaction was uniform: unheard of. Rapes were unheard of! Muggings were unheard of! People liked to blame such crimes on the Korean troops in town. The Korean troops were tough, God knows. But they were hardly responsible for as much as people required.

This also was when I saw American armed forces I did not recognize. Posters espousing racial or ethnic contentiousness appeared at the Enlisted Men's Club at Ton Son Nhut. Panthers, Many Smokes Native Americans, La Raza. If all these enmities had been practiced in the field it would have been a horror story. They were not, out in the line. They were, in the barracks, at Bien Hoa and Long Binh Jail. There, robberies of marines by marines, sailors by sailors, all over the country at the big bases. Just like the robberies of Ford assembly-line workers in Dearborn, Michigan, by other line workers during the same era. All against all. Years before, I had regarded my uniform as an absurdity. Now I felt proud to have worn it, and ashamed.

Drugs were everywhere in the military, among enlisted personnel and among officers. People like Lieutenant Calley, who presided over the massacre at My Lai, were being commissioned. It was over.

I was leaving. I was glad I had not succeeded in getting over for Lam Son 719. I regretted I had not. Waiting for my Air Vietnam bus on Tu Do Street, I saw that the day of my flight out would be like the day of my arrival. The sky was black with monsoon clouds, lightning broke with Olympian force. At Ton Son Nhut there was a crazy American soldier staring at people. His uniform was unbuttoned and no one seemed to be in charge of him. He walked from person to person, from group to group, staring, furious. You could see people waiting for civilian transport out wondering whether this demented soldier was going to attack them.

Is this how I'm going to die here? You could see people wondering that, I'm sure of it. After everything, is this crazy GI going to kill me?

A couple of hours later I was in Bangkok, the Bangkok of the Orient. I had bought a bathing suit at a shop down Phya Thai Road, the smallest size I could find. It was much too big for me. When I dived into the pool, the suit came off and floated around my ankles. When I surfaced, everyone in the place was convulsed with laughter. The Japanese businessmen seated at the pool's edge, the senior female executives from the sex industry, the Korean tourists—all, all burst into applause. I paddled to where I could stand up, climbed into the trunks, and waddled out of the pool.

The next morning I left for the Buddhist monastery at Ayutthaya. In a temple beside it, a gargantuan gold-painted Buddha contemplated with an antique smile the farmers and fishermen imploring his compassion. Around the monastery, monks drank beer like Friar Tuck. Small boys in saffron robes with shaved heads scampered through the silkwood branches. I obtained and drank a bottle of Mekong whiskey.

"Weakness of the strong man," the chief monk said merrily as he prodded me awake. For a place pledged to Lady Poverty, they were charging me quite a lot for a few days' lodging.

"There it is," I said. Who knew what I meant by that? It was what everybody said in Vietnam when they thought they had glimpsed the dark antic spirit of the war.

Two days before I left, a monk tied a saffron band around my wrist. I stopped drinking and spent a night in meditation. I drew breath to the reverberation of gongs. On the flight back to London I still heard them. I had acquired a taste for the examined life and focused on my saffron band. A woman beside me—a tourist, I suppose—sat fidgeting in the next seat. Finally I turned toward her and presented a friendly aspect. She asked me whence I had come and whither I was bound. At the word *Vietnam* she froze.

"I hope you had nothing to do with the war."

"Very little," I told her. And to my own surprise, I cut her dead for the rest of the trip.

EPILOGUE

During the four years of our expatriation in England, news came to us through the distanced lens of foreign media. History seemed America-driven, occurring—exploding—across the Atlantic or in reaction to some scheme hatched there.

The shaken newsagent on West Heath Road who sold us the *Guardian* headlining the murder of Martin Luther King seemed about to say something beyond "k'yew" as he folded the paper and handed it to us. Or rather, as my wife, who actually bought the paper from him, said, he seemed to be waiting for us to say something. We had nothing to say, however, no words of illumination, no comment. Nor could we shed light on the pattern of riots that beset the country in the wake of the murder or the assassin's extended evasion of arrest.

And in north Wales a few months later, a boy ran into our parlor from the rolling, sheep-razed meadow outside, shouting and waving the morning's newspaper: "Robert Kennedy is dead, look!"

Shot, of course, whacked in the American manner. We could not be helpful. Sorry. Guns are pretty easy to get in the U.S.; if you really want one you can get it. So if you want to shoot someone and take no thought for the morrow, you can figure out a way to do it. This should have been well known to readers of the British press of any age by then.

One principle of international reportage familiar to any traveler or expatriate must be that newspapers try to tell their readers what those readers believe they already know about the countries reported on. Rarely do stories appear in which Frenchmen, Britons, Americans, Germans, Russians, et cetera behave in a manner utterly different from the national character that has been established for them (no doubt with a degree of their own collaboration) by decades of journalistic vaudeville, cartoons, and accent comedy. This is only one aspect of the newspaper business strategy of making a reader feel as knowledgeably at home in the great world as he is in his favorite living-room chair.

Vietnam dominated the international picture to such an extent that classically attuned commentators compared it to the Athenian expedition against Syracuse. Athens destroyed its democracy in the course of besieging, at great cost, a stubborn Spartan ally. Along with democracy, it sacrificed its reputation for probity and wise policy, and its treasure. In the analogy, the United States was cast as Athens.

I thought that if I went to Vietnam as a veteran of the American military, living in Europe and sufficiently liberated from America's imagining of its own blameless and heroic role in Asia, I might learn a few things. I would be going, after all, as the correspondent of a British publication. As it happened, the publication went out of business while I was still there, and I ended up writing mainly about bar scenes and rock concerts.

However, I got around a bit, enough to see that answers to some questions—such as those concerning the moral justification for a war—are better pursued through the techniques of fiction than through any work a reporter can do. For one thing, facts unexamined can be made to subvert fundamental truth. Questions of this sort can be debated endlessly. But the intersection of facts and the truth was one of the problematic junctures I learned something about in Vietnam, which, I believe, made my going worthwhile.

I saw some unpleasant aspects of the United States in Vietnam that were familiar to me from home. I had never witnessed them brought to bear on such a scale. The war had distended them into a mistake ten thousand miles long, technologized beyond anyone's control. I will say I never saw anything in Vietnam that deeply scandalized me as an American, though I know that others did. From my own time in the military I knew a few things about military villainy and brutality that under the pressure of inept or desperate leadership can lead to inhuman behavior.

Much of the time, my wife and I thought, it didn't matter where we lived. Our children, by default, became beneficiaries and victims of our principal life decisions. But going to Vietnam had in fact made me curious enough about America, its conditions, and the manner in which it contrived to live at home—while purporting to export a way of life desirable for all humanity.

Considering our next move, we listened to the available wisdom. A few weeks after I got back from Ton Son Nhut, Janice and I were flying over the Mediterranean coast of France. Our pilot, whose private plane it was, was a woman who had lived for many years in Provence. When I told her that we were deciding whether to return to America or not, her reaction was so intense that for a moment I thought something had gone wrong with the aircraft's engine. There was nothing wrong. Only that she felt strongly that we should not take our children to America, where they would become Americans.

Back in London, I met a visiting professor from Princeton University, Edmund Keeley, who offered me a teaching position for the 1971–72 academic year. I decided to accept. That amounted to deciding on permanent return. Our children, aged eight and eleven, having spent four years in London, were indistinguishable from London children of the middle class.

At a party thrown by one of our neighbors, I decided to announce what it seemed would become of us.

"We'll take them back," I said. "They're American. They should know that that's what they are. It's a great thing to be British. But I think they should know their Americanness. Live there. Have the experience." And so on, said I.

My neighbors were cool, by which I mean they were poised and polite. Only for the fraction of a moment did the face of the man I was speaking to fix itself in shock. Then he blinked and was at ease.

"Oh, absolutely," he said.

The other people in the room had also fallen silent for a second or two. They too rallied quickly.

"No question!"

"Of course. They must."

It is certainly true that our neighbors, good sports all, from the days of Ken Kesey's visit to the day we departed, were probably not too distressed at the prospect of a little more quiet in the building. But in fact I think they were truly disturbed at what they saw as our wrongheadedness, the mistake we were about to make, the deprivation to which we intended to subject our children.

The day we got back to the United States the governor of New York State quelled a prison riot by shooting down the rebellious prisoners and the guards they had taken hostage. Nelson Rockefeller looked pretty bad after that, but no one looked good. Not the politicians who seized the opportunity of the riot to advance their faces and fortunes. Not the radical lawyers who had encouraged the prisoners to continue their mutiny by falsely assuring them that representatives of the Third World were en route by UN helicopters to spirit them away to sanctuary. Everyone lied, there were killings. More to be sure than were "necessary."

The California of our youth, whose very name was magic, had been transformed into a neat industrial landscape. The orchards that had not been good enough for us as we found them, that we had felt the need to illuminate and gild with the wine of astonishment and hang with acid lilacs, were orchards no more, they were Silicon Valley. Their magic was artificial intelligence, the terrifying stuff Professor Lederberg had warned us against long before.

Some of the changes we had hoped for, that we had professed to see even then mystically resolving the imbalances of the old worn imperfect world, had been hammered halfway into place with much compromise and considerable ill will. The drugs which we believed so important a part of our liberation, the key to the music, the doors of perception for an elite, became a mass youth phenomenon. They caused much suffering and parental anguish, and they forged a weapon for the use of the darkest forces in American society, the witch-hunting, punitive-minded hypocrites who promptly gave us the War on Drugs as they had given us Prohibition.

As young bohemians with artistic pretensions we used drugs in imitation of the European decadents. We may not have had any choice, but in the end we allowed drugs to be turned into a weapon against everything we believed in.

Admittedly, we imagined ourselves, we students in California and such places, as an elite. By providing the enemies of freedom and insight with a drug menace to hype in their yellow press, we gave aid and comfort to the greatest argument for elitism since Edmund Burke went to Parliament—American populism, notorious as a pious front for venal corruption, the curse of this nation, and now, empowered by American wealth and resources, a worldwide plague.

To the bleating of their politicians and preachers, the venal populists were able to turn a provision of the health code into an immeasurably costly game of cops and robbers that made our difficulties with drugs, a marginal problem in most civilized countries, into an endless pep rally for repression of all sorts.

My generation left the country better in some ways, not least by destroying the letter of the laws of racism and sexual discrimination. We were one of the generations to which the word "Romantic" might be applied—the offspring of a period inclined by history to highly value the Dionysian and the spontaneous, to exalt freedom over order, to demand more of the world than it may reasonably provide. We saw—may we not be the last to see—this country as blessed in its most generous hopes.

The Road was the revered totem of our generation. The teeming Open Road, the idea of it, was beloved of poets such as Whitman, Ginsberg, and Kerouac. Ken Kesey too. It signified optimism, joyous expectation, an anticipation of the best in possibility. It embraced risk in an attitude of faith that looked forward to the advancement of everything within us that was nobler, more generous, and more just.

Our expectations were too high, our demands excessive; things were harder than we expected. Kesey's wise maxim about offering more than what he could deliver, in order to deliver what he could, described his life's efforts—and not only his. It is true, I believe, of every person, or any group of people who ever set out to advance anything beyond their own personal advantage. We must believe in the efficacy of our own efforts. Maybe we have to believe in it to the point of excess. Excess is always a snare for those who demand much from themselves or from life. Excess, in fact, is characteristic of romantics, of romantic generations.

In our time, we were clamorous and vain. I speak not only for myself here, but for all those with whom I shared the era and what I think of as its attitudes. We wanted it all; sometimes we confused self-destructiveness with virtue and talent, obliteration with ecstasy, heedlessness with courage. Worshipping the doctrines of Hemingway as we did, we wanted constant grace under constant pressure, and stoicism before a disillusionment that somehow never went stale. We wanted to die well every single day, to be a cool guy and a good-looking corpse. How absurd, because nothing is free, and we had to learn that at last. Every generation must—be it romantic or pragmatic, spiritually striving or materialistic as a copper penny. We learned what we had to, and we did what we could. In some ways the world profited and will continue to profit by what we succeeded in doing. We were the chief victims of our own mistakes. Measuring ourselves against the masters of the present, we regret nothing except our failure to prevail.